D0864671

THE HOLY SPIRIT~
SHY MEMBER
OF THE
TRINITY

THE HOLY SPIRIT~
SHY MEMBER
OF THE
TRINITY

Frederick Dale Bruner
and William Hordern

AUGSBURG Publishing House • Minneapolis

THE HOLY SPIRIT—SHY MEMBER OF THE TRINITY

Scripture quotations unless otherwise noted are from the Revised Standard Version of the Bible, copyright 1946, 1952, and 1971 by the Division of Christian Education of the National Council of Churches.

Library of Congress Cataloging in Publication Data

Bruner, Frederick Dale.
    THE HOLY SPIRIT, SHY MEMBER OF THE TRINITY.

    Includes bibliographical references.
    1. Holy Spirit—Addresses, essays, lectures.
I. Hordern, William. II. Title.
BT122.B75   1984   231'.3   83-72124
ISBN 0-8066-2068-4 (pbk.)

Manufactured in the U.S.A.   APH 10-3070

1 2 3 4 5 6 7 8 9 0 1 2 3 4 5 6 7 8 9

Contents

Preface

For several years the churches of North America have been torn by debate over the Holy Spirit. How is the Holy Spirit received and what are the marks of the Holy Spirit's presence? Are some believers more filled with the Spirit than others? In response to such questions, the authors have tried to look at the biblical understanding of the Spirit with the modern situation in mind.

For example, some teach that the coming of the Spirit occurs mainly in prayer meetings, where hands are laid on seekers and where the Spirit's full coming is evidenced by speaking in tongues (see Richard Quebedeaux, *The New Charismatics II,* Harper and Row, 1983, pp. 147-150). This book presents the conviction that, according to the New Testament and the continuing history of the church, the Holy Spirit comes in fullness, again and again, through the hearing of the

Christian sermon with faith. This is not opposed to prayer meetings; it creates them.

The authors do not believe that there is any other gospel (for example, a "full gospel") than the simple gospel of faith in Christ. To believe in Christ *is* the filling of the Spirit, and every new draft of faith in the Savior is a fresh filling of the Spirit. We do not disagree with repeated fillings of the Spirit; we disagree only with those who say that there must be a *second* (or in holiness churches, a third) crisis-encounter with God before believers are finally filled with the Spirit.

These essays on the Holy Spirit attempt to honor the gospel, by contrasting it with current teachings that dishonor the gospel by making it only preliminary. We do not claim to teach new truth about the Holy Spirit, but we do attempt to teach the gospel in a fresh way. This is possible because false doctrines have enabled the church to appreciate the gospel from a new angle.

If spiritism is one error to be avoided, "triumphalism" is the other. Every Nicene Christian believes that a part of the gospel is the victory that Christ gives over evil spirits. But how this victory is obtained, lived, and evidenced is a subject of disagreement in the churches. There are contemporary "theologies of glory" that do end runs around the suffering of the cross and promise Christians direct access to the power of the resurrection. These theologies take many forms, but they all unite in their focus on power by technique. Against these new triumphalisms, so widespread in the electronic church, but also popular in many Christian churches, movements, and books, the authors propose the Reformation "theology of the cross." In the theology of the cross, failure is often God's way of succeeding, thorns in the flesh are often Christ's way of equipping us with power, and little, honest churches are often more liberating than vast popular movements. "When I am weak, then I am strong" (2 Cor. 12:10).

To sum up, we believe that preaching the gospel is the way of the Spirit's fullness, even in late 20th-century Christendom, against all charismatic spiritisms and new revelations; and bearing the cross is the way Christians live lives of resurrection power, against the many culture-religions of success, prosperity, and easy victories.

The gospel of Jesus Christ is still its own best defense and needs no outside help. The theology of the cross, which owes its name (but not its truth) to Luther, and which is as old and as apostolic as the gospel according to Mark and to Paul, is still a clear optic on the Christian life and a means by which to describe the person and work of the Holy Spirit today.

Garrett–Evangelical Theological Seminary was the pleasant venue of these Franklin Hall Lectures for 1982. Professor William Richard Stegner was especially helpful to us both in careful preparations and in many personal helps—from the lectures to this book. President Neil Fisher was very gracious. It may be a source of ecumenical encouragement to know that a classically Methodist seminary welcomed the teachings of a Lutheran (William Hordern) and a Presbyterian (F. Dale Bruner) on the Holy Spirit. It was a pleasant surprise to this Lutheran and Presbyterian (in our work here for the first time together) that our views so frequently converged, not least in the vexed area of the sacraments. We want to thank our Methodist brothers and sisters at Garrett–Evangelical Theological Seminary for making this whole enterprise both possible and happy.

May this book bring glory to the Holy Spirit, who lives to give glory to Jesus Christ, who lived, died, lives, and will come again to give glory to God the Father.

1 The Shy Member of the Trinity

Expository Preaching Gives the Filling of the Holy Spirit

F. Dale Bruner

A Christian wants to have every possible resource for living the Christian life. A Christian, by definition, wants to be christened by, or filled with, the Spirit. The desire for spiritual filling is particularly keen in those preparing for professional Christian ministry because the expectations of the people of God are so high and the needs of the world so deep. Ministers of the gospel (and serious disciples) are not only eager for their own filling with the Spirit, they also seek to be the means of their people's filling with the Spirit as well.

I want to address myself especially to these two seekings. First, how may we ourselves, as teachers and disciples, be filled with the Spirit? And, second, how may we be means of grace for our people in relation to the Spirit? I cannot pretend to be especially spiritual or to know special spiritual truths of or secrets about the

Spirit. But I can seek faithfully to teach the public data of Scripture and Christian tradition on the doctrine and experience of the Spirit.

The filling of the Spirit

Our enquiry is put beneath the proper star if I tell you at once the most helpful words I ever heard on this subject. Every Saturday evening while I was a student at Princeton Theological Seminary, a group of us visited with then 90-year-old biblical commentator Dr. Charles Erdman who lived across the street from the campus. Dr. Erdman was the Dr. William Barclay of my generation—that is, he had written a widely used set of popular commentaries on the entire New Testament, and that fact, along with Dr. Erdman's personal grace, gave us a sense that we could trust him to know God's Word and Spirit. Dr. Erdman had also been at church conferences with Charles Spurgeon, D. L. Moody, F. B. Meyer, and other worthies of the 19th-century church. We students felt that when we were talking with Dr. Erdman we were actually talking with the 19th-century evangelical church, and it was exciting. The most memorable Saturday evening visit of all was the evening we discussed the Holy Spirit. I still recall Dr. Erdman's reply to a question about how one could be filled with the Holy Spirit according to the New Testament and according to Dr. Erdman's own experience as a Christian. He told us of the different answers he had received to this question as a student at the D. L.

Moody Northfield Conferences, and of how he had been more than a little confused on the subject because one summer a speaker would give one set of conditions and the next summer quite a different set. Then Dr. Erdman said something I have never forgotten, and to this day I call it "Erdman's Law." This was what he said: "I have become convinced that those persons are most filled with the Holy Spirit who are least conscious of it; all they know is that they wish to serve Jesus Christ, and they feel that they are unprofitable servants." I think this means that if you and I are Christians who want to believe and obey the Jesus Christ of Scripture in the world of today, and if you and I are seriously discontented with our faith and obedience and long to be better Christians, we are not devoid of the Spirit, but we are actually filled with the Spirit. *Being* filled with the Spirit is often a different thing than *feeling* filled. Dr. Erdman said that the persons whom he had known and admired as Christians in his long ministry would have been surprised to have been described as Spirit-filled persons. Rather, he said, simply wanting to serve Christ well was itself the great evidence of the filling of the Spirit. This is good news, since our normal sense of self as Christians—I think I can speak for most of us—is a sense of great inadequacy.

I believe that Erdman's Law ("those persons are most filled with the Spirit who are least conscious of it") is a faithful reproduction of the New Testament teaching on the Holy Spirit. It is a relief to know, is it not, that we can be normal, struggling Christian men and women and still be filled with the Spirit. It is not necessary for us to glow in the dark or be radiant with victory in order for us to be God's servants and be experiencing (even against our experience) the power of God's Spirit. The words, "Blessed are the poor in spirit," Jesus' opening teaching words in the gospel of Matthew (5:3), have more than one meaning. In fact, these words come as close to saying the essential thing on the subject of the Holy Spirit as they do on several other subjects. "Blessed are the poor in spirit, for theirs is the kingdom of heaven" is simply said in another way when we paraphrase, "Blessed are the poor in spirit, for theirs is the filling of the Spirit." To want the Spirit is to have the Spirit. Luther's famous formula applies here too: *"Glaubst du, so hast du"* ("Believe, and you've got it").

One of the most surprising discoveries in my own study of the doctrine and experience of the Spirit in the New Testament is what I can only call the shyness of the Spirit, a thesis that I will document in a moment. Could it be that one reason why the persons who, in Dr. Erdman's conviction, were filled with the Spirit were shy about their filling was the fact that the very Spirit of God is shy? What I mean here by shyness is not the shyness of timidity (cf. 2 Tim. 1:7), but the shyness of deference, the shyness of a concentrated centering of attention on another; it is not the shyness (such as we often experience) of self-centeredness, but the shyness of an other-centeredness. It is a shyness, if I

14

may put it this way, like the relation of Ed McMahon to Johnny Carson. It is, in a word, the shyness of tact. Consider the way that the Jesus of John's gospel bears witness to the special work of the coming Holy Spirit, noting particularly the personal pronouns in order to make the point as clear as possible:

"The Counselor, the Holy Spirit, whom the Father will send in *my* name, he will teach you all things, and bring to your remembrance all that *I* have said to you. . . . When the Counselor comes, . . . he will bear witness to *me*. . . . And when he comes, he will [convict] the world concerning sin . . . because they do not believe in *me* . . . When the Spirit of truth comes . . . he will not speak on his own authority, but whatever he hears he will speak. . . . He will glorify *me,* for he will take what is *mine* and declare it to you" (John 14:26; 15:26; 16:8f., 13f.; italics added).

The work of the *Holy* Spirit is the honoring of Jesus Christ. The work of other spirits is the honoring of themselves or of other realities. We are not necessarily in the presence of the Holy Spirit when we are in the presence of a great deal of talk about the Holy Spirit. But wherever a church or a person centers thoughtfully (that is, biblically and evangelically) on honoring the person, teaching, and work of Jesus Christ, there, we may be quite sure, we are in the presence of the Holy Spirit. For the Spirit's work is the thoughtful honoring of Christ. The Holy Spirit does not center on the Holy Spirit. That is the clear teaching of Jesus in John's gospel and elsewhere.

15

It has often been said that the Holy Spirit is the Cinderella of the Trinity, the great neglected person of the Godhead, and that if the church could rediscover the person and work of the Holy Spirit, it would, at the same time, rediscover the power of Pentecost and of the earliest Christians. I am not convinced. While Dr. Hordern and I will seek to honor the person and work of the Holy Spirit in this book and to clear a larger place in our thought for a sense of the Spirit's work in our ministries, I do not honestly believe that a new Spirit-centeredness is what our churches need.[1] I do believe, however, that the Spirit's sign, desire, and work is that we be overcome again, thrilled again, excited, impressed, and gripped again by the wonder, the majesty, the earthiness, and the relevance of Jesus and his Word to our world. The Holy Spirit does not mind being Cinderella outside the ballroom if the Prince is honored inside his Kingdom. For the Holy Spirit is really the shy member of the Trinity.

Luke's Jesus put it this way to the disciples just before Pentecost: "But you shall receive power when the Holy Spirit has come upon you; and [then] you shall be *my* witnesses," witnesses to *me* in the whole wide world (Acts 1:8, italics added). When the Holy Spirit comes upon waiting disciples, they become witnesses, not to the Holy Spirit, but to Jesus Christ—"you shall be *my* witnesses," Jesus promised.

To help me dramatize what I believe the Holy Spirit's work is, according to the New Testament, imagine my drawing a stick-figure of Jesus of Nazareth on the

16

chalkboard. After drawing Jesus on the board, I then impersonate the Spirit, stepping behind the board and pointing only my index finger in front of the board in the direction of the picture of Jesus. Then I say, urgently and insistently, "Look at him!" That is the work of the Holy Spirit. The Spirit stands *behind* the board urging what is *on* the board. The Spirit is most present where Jesus is most central. The Spirit does not mind being neglected if Jesus is not. (This may be one answer to the question of why there are so few references to the Spirit in the synoptic Gospels.) I do not believe that the church needs a new focus on the Spirit in order to be renewed, because the Spirit's work is to focus the church's attention ever and again on quite another center.

Reformation theology in the 16th century and New Reformation theology in the 20th century have been criticized for being "unitarianisms of the second person of the Trinity," that is, for concentrating too much on Christ and insufficiently on God the Father and on God the Spirit. But I do not think the criticism is deserved. Where the Jesus of the New Testament is faithfully exposited through the texts where Jesus appears, there God the Father and God the Spirit are almost always covered with glory. For example, the historical Jesus is what we may call shy, too, in the presence of the one whom he most often calls his Father. "Why do you call me good?" he said on one well-known occasion; "No one is good but God alone" (Mark 10:18). Jesus did not want to shine at the Father's expense. Jesus is transparent to God, focused on God, the God-intoxicated man, and there is no single encounter with Jesus in the New Testament or in life that does not also resonate with the depth of a contact with God. (This God-experiencing reality is partly due to the simple fact of the full deity of Jesus Christ; it is partly due as well to the emphasis of Jesus' historical teaching ministry and his mission in the world—to glorify God.) Jesus, too, is shy.

Jesus also defers to the Holy Spirit. In the gospel of Mark, Jesus says that while every blasphemy uttered by the sons of men will be forgiven, blasphemy against the Holy Spirit will never be forgiven (3:28-30); thus Jesus gives pride of place to the Spirit—to the very Spirit whose mission it is that Jesus be given pride of place.

Finally, to complicate the picture thoroughly, we have the witness of the one called God the Father in the Gospels. It is well known that this God speaks directly to earth only twice in the synoptic Gospels—at Jesus' baptism and at Jesus' transfiguration. Both times this God says the same thing, and at the Mount of Transfiguration three words are added. Here, then, is the total *direct* witness of God the Father to Jesus according to Matthew, Mark, and Luke: "And a voice came from heaven, saying, 'This is my priceless Son, I am deeply pleased with him,' [adding, at the transfiguration], 'Listen to *him!*'" (Matt. 3:17; 17:5; author's translation).[2] What this voice means is this: the major fact, bar none, that God the Father wants the world to know is all that we have in his Son. Jesus of

Nazareth is the almost total preoccupation, if I may put it that way, of the God of the synoptic Gospels. It is worth noticing that the voice from heaven does not say, for example, "Listen to me, too, after listening to him; don't forget that I'm here, too; don't be too taken up with my Son." God the Father is shy, too. The whole blessed Trinity is shy. Each member of the Trinity points faithfully and selflessly to the other in a gracious circle.

Where, then, do we focus our attention? The New Testament is very clear about this: We focus our attention on Jesus of Nazareth, who himself keeps us wholesomely trinitarian. Where the Christ of the prophetic and apostolic Scriptures is evangelically central—and by that I mean, where the Scriptures are explained, as they were intended to be, paragraph by paragraph, in a rigorous lifetime program of evangelical expository preaching and teaching—there will be no one-sided unitarianism of the second person of the Trinity, but there will be evangelical-catholic trinitarianism. Our theologies, our churches, and our own ministries are only then skewed, one-sided, and misleading when we fail to bring all our teaching, all of Scripture, and all our people into their God-intended focus on Christ, the Son of God. "Listen to *him!*"

Conservative-evangelical theology is sometimes too independently interested in the Bible itself—in biblical inerrancy, biblical biographies, and biblical facts—or, alternatively, in human hearts, human decisions, and human spiritual struggles. The result is that conservative evangelism often misses the point of the Bible and the human, and that point is Jesus Christ, the Lord. The Bible is not about the Bible.

On the other hand, liberal and liberation theologies are sometimes too independently interested in the world and in strategies for the world's renewal, or, alternatively, in radical personalities and programs. The result is that they often miss the only responsible way to renewal and the genuinely radical, namely, faith in Christ the liberator, in the fellowship of his always-problematic church. If we follow the lead of the biblical Holy Spirit, we will make it the chief aim of our ministries that Jesus Christ be heard, received, and obeyed—then and only then is the biblical Word rightly used in the church; then and only then is the secular world served intelligently by the church and by its people in the world.

There is, therefore, no tricky way to the filling of the Holy Spirit. There is simply believing Jesus Christ; there is only believing Jesus as he is ministered to us in the preaching, sacraments, fellowship, and prayer life of our churches. There is no full gospel other than the simple gospel—the good news, that is, that Jesus is what the world needs.

How, then, may one be filled with the Holy Spirit? I can paraphrase Paul's answer to the Philippian jailer's similar question about salvation and give the correct answer: "Believe in the Lord Jesus, and you will be ~~filled with the Spirit~~, you and your whole house" (cf. Acts 16:31).

saved
NIV

20

The mediation of the Spirit

The Spirit is mediated to the people of God when pastors, teachers, and people so present Jesus Christ to others that faith is awakened. In the New Testament, there is one way to the filling of the Spirit, the simple way of Christocentricity (or Christopistics, "faith-in-Christ-ness"). Usually the spiritual life of the people of God in our parishes only rises as high, and the people's social outreach only extends as far, as the height and the breadth of the preaching ministry of the pastors. (Since I am not ordained, my honoring of the preaching ministry in these essays should not be seen as self-serving. I do teach Sunday school regularly.)

Of course, the Spirit is mediated in a whole host of mysterious and unmysterious ways, known and unknown to us. "The wind blows where it wills . . . so it is with . . . the Spirit" (John 3:8). We know that the ordinary life of the faithful Christian people in the world is a mighty mediation of the Spirit. But I am addressing the Christian ministry in particular here, and in the New Testament this ministry is especially a ministry of Word and sacrament.

Whether we like the fact or not, the Sunday morning sermon has been the ordinary conduit of the life-giving Spirit to the people of God through the ages. (I will make a lot of this fact.) Where pastors have made it their aim to glorify God as revealed in Christ by Scripture and thus have helped to move their people out into God's wounded world by means of faithfulness in their several vocations, there, historically, men and

21

women have been filled with the power of the Spirit, there congregations have come alive, and there people have gone into their communities in intelligent witness, service, and conflict. The great desire of the Holy Spirit is that our churches so exalt Jesus Christ that men and women are moved to God through Christ, become his disciples in the fellowship of the churches, and then follow him into adventuresome service and controversy in the world.

Deflection from this Christocentric, missiocentric focus is, in my own reading of Scripture and in my own experience, deflection into the death of irrelevance or busyness. We want to be excited by Jesus Christ all over again. When I was in college and preparing for Christian mission, one of my pastors told me, "Dale, pray for the amateur spirit." He meant, pray for a continued sense of excitement by the theme of Scripture, which is Christ. The great professional hazard for us who study and teach Holy Scripture is the hazard of the insider's boredom with the theme, the hazard of the ho-hum of familiarity. We need to hear again and again the voice of God the Father, "This is my priceless Son. I am deeply pleased with him."

One big contribution of the apostle Paul is his gift for making us feel spiritually poor and emotionally cold toward Christ and his mission. Unlike us, Paul is always "hot," and one of his best ministries is making one feel bad. Paul knows, in his words, that "all the treasures of wisdom and knowledge are hid in Christ" (Col. 2:3). I remember the best expository teacher of

Scripture I ever had, my dear college Sunday school teacher, Dr. Henrietta Mears, say, "How can a preacher ever run out of themes to preach when his or her theme is, in Paul's words, 'the unsearchable riches of Christ' " (Eph. 3:8).

The work of the Holy Spirit is simply to thrill us with Christ, to infect us with enthusiasm for all that Christ can do for men and women and for the world to change things, to renew institutions, and to salvage lives. The Holy Spirit is shy about absolutely everything except Christ, but about Christ the Spirit is downright bullish. Matthew, Mark, Luke, John, Paul, Peter, and all the rest were united in one great fact: they believed that Jesus was central, and they never stopped pushing him. Irenaeus, Athanasius, Chrysostom, Augustine, Anselm, Thomas, Luther, Calvin, Bengel, Wesley, Schlatter, and Barth all shared this Christ-passion with the apostles. They shared a common enthusiasm for the raw relevance of Jesus to the deepest needs of human life and society. More than anything else, they cared that Jesus be preached, believed, and obeyed. And that caring is exactly what it means to be filled with the Holy Spirit: "Here is God's priceless Son, with whom God is deeply pleased. Listen to him!"

It is the great work of the Spirit, then, that Christ be known. Therefore, when we too make this our great work, we find ourselves filled with the Spirit whose great work this is. We make this our work (speaking now very practically to seminary students and pastors) when we determine to preach Christ out of the Hebrew and Greek texts of our Scriptures or, if one prefers, out of a deep study of the Bible in the mother tongue.[3] Preaching and teaching that is born of a prayerful wrestling with the biblical texts in an almost athletic attempt each week to find the *real* meaning of these authoritative scriptural sentences—*that* is evangelical-catholic preaching and teaching. Such preaching and teaching is, when it pleases God to honor it, filled with the Spirit.

On the other hand, a regular diet of topical sermons is very like the Antichrist, for regular topical preaching is the death of the church. Sermons, Sunday school lessons, and church education materials that are merely thematic and do not say in modern words what the prophets and apostles said in their inspired words are more like the beast of Revelation than the blessing of the Gospels. Enthusiasm for Christ today is responsible, not fanatic, when it is a zeal to say what the biblical writers really said about Christ, a zeal to repeat in fresh words what the apostles or prophets actually wrote; it is the determination to interpret with absolute honesty what every paragraph in the Scriptures really *says*. For most preaching pastors, the hard road of Hebrew and Greek exegesis is a main highway into a ministry filled with the Spirit. Let us forget every other priority in seminary until we read our Bibles daily and devotionally in the biblical languages, until our every sermon and lesson is the full translation, in words and spirit, of a paragraph of Scripture. Then both we and our people will be in the free windstream of the Spirit, who inspired and still inspires Scripture. If it is true that theology is the complex science of keeping the gospel from becoming complex, then it is also true that evangelical exegesis-and-exposition is the "unsimple" science of keeping the gospel both simple and unsimplistic.[4]

The name of what I am urging as the most responsible means for the pastoral mediation of the Spirit is the eight-letter word *exegesis*. This word is the best word I know for encouraging seminarians and pastors to be the means of their peoples' filling with the Spirit. If believing Christ is the way we ourselves are filled with the Spirit (and we are not allowed to make filling with the Spirit any more complex than faith), then interpreting Scripture is usually the main way that pastors are means of grace to the greater part of their people each week (and we are not allowed to make the minister's mediation of the Spirit any less complex than exegesis).

I am in danger of two errors here. First, of a technology of the Spirit, i.e., a set of techniques guaranteed to deliver the Holy Spirit. This would involve me in what the late President John Mackay of Princeton Seminary used to call the prostitution of God. God the Holy Spirit is free, and not even our best exegesis or most devout prayer or life can ever guarantee the Spirit's real presence. The Spirit blows where she wills (John 3:8).[5]

Second, I am in danger of committing the error of imposing what I love on others. I love exegesis. But

25

exegesis may not be every pastor's or teacher's main gift (1 Corinthians 12). Am I wrong, however, in believing that exegesis is almost every preacher's, and many church teachers', main *responsibility?* (See, e.g., the pastoral parable, Matt. 24:45-51, and especially v. 45c: "giving them their food in season." What is this food but the gospel of Scripture? And what is this season but the Spirit's application of the gospel to the situation?) When these two dangers—spiritual technology and charismatic manipulation—have been noted, I believe it is appropriate to press hard for serious biblical exposition in the churches as the ordinary medium of God's gift of the Spirit to the people. To be sure, Christianity is much more than a Word-event, but it is nothing less. *Many* more things than preaching should happen in and through churches — but will they be healthy happenings, or even happen at all, without responsible preaching? Not often. Karl Barth's *Church Dogmatics,* I/1-2, are continual and convincing rehearsal of the fundamental truth of the church's *(a)* Christocentric *(b)* biblical *(c)* preaching as the triune form of the one Word of God to the world.

We are not preaching God's Word when we are not explaining God's words. The Holy Scriptures are God's words (plural); Jesus Christ is God's Word (singular); and preaching can be defined as human words about God's words about God's Word. If we are being more than poetic when we say that Scriptures are actually God's words in human words, then why do we preach anything else? I think regular topical or thematic

26

preaching is acted-out unbelief; it is the perhaps unconscious denial of the church's perennial conviction that Scripture is God's written Word. For if we believed that Scripture is, as it is, the inerrant Word of God written with errant human words, we would not give ourselves to anything else than to trying to paraphrase and proclaim this Word for our time. God has spoken, and in Jesus of Nazareth he has said his last word. He has nothing else to say. He is spoken out. (What God *is saying* now is paracletic interpretation of what he *said* then in Jesus, John 14–16.) The historical Jesus is what God is *all* about, as the voice at Jesus' baptism and transfiguration makes pellucidly clear. Then why should we try, at bottom, to make anything else known? For when Jesus is made known in all his regal and crucified fullness, the Spirit is at once both the source and the gift of that making known, and so discipleship happens, and so the world changes.

The world knows how to do many things better than the church, and we do well to follow the world's wisdom in a variety of matters. There is one thing the world does not know better or by itself, and that one thing only the church can tell it. That is the gospel— that God in Christ died for the world, that Jesus Christ now reigns as its Lord, as its judge, and (where it repents) as its liberator. Making this Jesus known to the world, in the power of the Spirit, is the great reason for the church's existence. Why try to do Ralph Nader's work for him when, by means of our preaching Christ and so releasing the Spirit, God can produce a thousand Naders? The world can and does give good ideas and help; only the evangelical exposition of Holy Scripture gives the good news that God uses to give the Holy Spirit; and we exist to proclaim this news (it is God's business, exclusively, to give the Spirit).

What does this disquisition about the primacy of evangelical expository preaching have to do with the ministry of the Holy Spirit? In my opinion, a great deal. The Holy Spirit wants, above all else, that Jesus be known in the world. The main way that Jesus is known in the world is by the faithful preaching and teaching of Scripture's gospel. Through the faithful preaching and teaching of the gospel, God has historically released his Spirit into the lives of the believing church. In other words, to put it quite plainly, pastors are God's main plan of action in the world (see Calvin's great chapter, *Institutes,* IV. i). It is simply a church-historical fact that God uses ministers in a very special way in the building up of his church. Where the ministry is faithful in preaching, the people are filled with the Spirit. God fills men and women with the Spirit by means of pastors when they preach Jesus Christ faithfully, that is, when they preach Christ according to Holy Scripture's real meanings and the world's real needs. In the Reformation tradition we do not believe that the Spirit ordinarily comes to people apart from the ministry of Word and sacraments. A spirit unclothed by the Word (e.g., meeting for prophesying and testimony without gospel teaching) is nude and dangerous; the Word unclothed by the Spirit (e.g., even biblical exegesis without centering on the *gospel* of the Bible) is cold and even killing. The Spirit through the Word is sufficient and apostolic—*Holy* Spirit.

Gerhard Ebeling, in his now-published lectures to the University of Zürich on Luther, asked how it happened, historically, that Luther's Reformation, in contrast to the many prior attempts at church reformation in the Middle Ages, became a reformation in deed and not just in words; that is, how it became a world-changing reformation. Ebeling's reply is paradoxical and deep. Luther's Reformation, he writes, became a reformation in deed, not just in words because Luther trusted only in the Word and not at all in deeds.[6] Luther believed that sermons were God's main means for reforming the church and so for changing the world. He believed this, not because he had mystic trust in the power of spoken words, but because he knew his Bible and its teaching of the breathtaking power of the Word of Christ. The Jesus of John's gospel says it best of all: "The words I have spoken to you bring God's life-giving Spirit" (John 6:63, TEV; notice the two verbs: the christic perfect is the vehicle of the pneumatic present). The centurion said it well, too, speaking to Jesus: "Just say the word, and my servant will be well" (Matt. 8:8).

The Holy Spirit comes into the lives of men and women through the means of grace. At the head of these means, as the major means, is the exaltation of the Word and person of Jesus Christ, and so, of the Holy Trinity, through the faithful, evangelical exposi-

29

tion of Scripture. Paul wrote that "faith comes by hearing, and hearing by the preaching of Christ" (Rom. 10:17; see the community-building importance of Paul's not saying that faith comes by reading, i.e., privately).[7] In the same way the Holy Spirit, according to Paul, comes through the message of faith and not through our doing, even our doing of the best things, not even our doing God's will in the law (Gal. 3:2-5). (Even exegesis understood as a good work guaranteeing the Spirit is misconceived.) We are perversely inclined to trust our doing of special things as the means of our receiving God's Spirit and, so, of God's renewal of the church. (Faith is a gift of God; so is a regenerating sermon. But a sermon is also a human responsibility.) Both the New Testament and the church's reformations have taught us that renewal comes through responsible (i.e., evangelical) preaching, through preaching the message of faith, through the good news. The good news is that it is by no doing of ours at all, but through believing that Jesus Christ did it all, that we receive the filling of the Spirit and that day after day, year after year, the church is miraculously transformed, spiritually renewed, and equipped for service in the world.

My concern is for all who desire to be ministers of this transforming, Spirit-giving Word. May I commend you to your Hebrew and Greek Bible studies, before all other studies, and to the study of that "great church history," which is the exposition of Scripture through the now almost 30 centuries of the teaching of

Scripture. May I commend you to a lifetime of cohabitation with texts in order to find their honest meanings, to a Sunday-by-Sunday commitment to speaking the honest truth about the words of God to the real needs of the people of God in the clearest, freshest possible words of contemporary men and women. Church history clearly teaches us that as you are faithful to the ministry of God's words about the Word, God has been wont, when and where it pleased him, to pour out his Spirit upon the people. But if we depend mainly on our creative words about the world's latest causes and movements, it is all over. Then we are no longer ministers of God's unsearchable riches in Christ as they are lavished on us in Holy Scripture; we are simply clever or progressive.[8]

I have always felt that the finest compact portrait of a living church in the New Testament is found in Acts 2:42, immediately after Pentecost: "And they [that is, the new believers, with the apostles and disciples] devoted themselves to the apostles' teaching and fellowship, to the breaking of bread and the prayers." There we have the four great means of grace in the church spelled out and placed side by side. First, at the head is the apostles' teaching; that is, today, the New Testament message. Second is fellowship (or sharing), literally, *koinonia,* which includes (intensively) group sharing and (extensively) the sharing of what we are and have with hurting people in ministries of what today we call social service and social justice. Third is the breaking of the bread, which is the sacramental

31

dimension, the serious commitment to regular participation in the Lord's Supper. Fourth are the prayers, that is, prayer meetings, the great lost art in our time. The prayer meeting, and not the Holy Spirit, is the real Cinderella of contemporary Christendom. Each of these four means of grace deserves exposition, but I have concentrated on the first here because it is first in the New Testament. (In the next chapter I become sacramental.) Where people continue steadfastly in the apostles' teaching, and where they sit reverently at the apostles' feet to hear the Word of Jesus in order to obey it, there Pentecost happens all over again and there people are filled afresh with the Holy Spirit. Many of us are products of such churches, and we will never be able to be grateful enough that our churches loved Jesus Christ and taught him.

The Holy Spirit, then, is shy about everything except Christ's gospel. The Spirit is at work spreading that gospel in the world at this very moment, and if we would be in the stream of the Spirit's work, a work that is going on now whether we are in it or not, we will give ourselves in a new, committed way to the understanding and the joyful evangelical transmitting of the prophets' and apostles' teaching in Scripture. We will study our Hebrew and Greek Bibles devotionally, daily, persistently, and with a will to uncover there the unsearchable riches of Christ for our people and their myriad needs. For the Holy Spirit comes to our people, first of all, through evangelical expository teaching.

In all four canonical gospels, Jesus literally "gave up

the Spirit" on the cross.[9] I understand Jesus' "giving" of the Spirit at the cross to summarize, in one classic and perhaps unconscious picture, exactly the way that the Spirit theologians of the New Testament — Paul, Luke, and John — teach the people of God that the Spirit fills the church and encounters the world.[10] And he cried out with a great voice and yielded up the spirit *(aphēken to pneuma)*" (Matt. 27:50). May we ourselves be conveyors of that "great voice" that echoes down the centuries, bringing new life to generation after generation. For the voice of Christ is the vehicle of the Spirit.

2 Of Water and the Spirit

Christian Baptism Is the Baptism in the Holy Spirit

F. Dale Bruner

The thesis of this chapter is that just as we receive all of God—Father, Son, and Holy Spirit—through faith in the preaching of Jesus Christ (the theme of the last chapter), so the same Jesus Christ is delivered to us through Christian Baptism. Christian Baptism is Baptism in the Holy Spirit. Some may find this chapter too sacramental, feeling that to honor Baptism is to dishonor the preaching of faith in Christ. I will try to show, however, that Christian sacramentalism, rightly understood, is Christian evangelicalism.

It is an interesting fact that no persons in the history of the church were as tenacious as the 16th-century Lutheran, Reformed, and Anglican Reformers in their insistence on faith alone in Christ alone as the one way of salvation—in their conviction, that is, that believers receive every spiritual blessing in the heavenly places through simple faith in Christ. At the same time, these

Reformers were second to none in their confidence in the efficacy of Christian Baptism, even for infants, as the place where God grants the people of God all the benefits of Christ, especially the twofold gift of plenary forgiveness of sins and plenary reception of the Spirit.

For several reasons, it is felt today by many Christians, even in the Reformation traditions, that if one insists on faith in Christ as evangelical center, then one cannot consistently believe in a Baptism that does things, least of all in an effective Baptism of infants. After an early attraction myself to what is called Believer Baptism, I have been convinced that it is precisely faith in Christ that has led the Catholic, Orthodox, and main Reformation churches to the treasuring of Baptism as a means of grace and not just a symbol of grace.

The New Testament has taught most of the churches most of the time that in Baptism God gives the church the gift of the Holy Spirit. I will seek to illustrate why and how by means of an interpretation of Matthew 3, the story of Jesus' own baptism.

In the third chapter of Matthew, John the Baptist is on the scene. He is hurling out the challenge to the people of Israel to turn their lives completely around because the kingdom of heaven is on its way to them, with wrath for those who are unreal and with restoration for those who receive his baptism honestly. It belongs to the uniqueness of John's ministry that, along with his challenge in words, John offers his hearers a place to show they accept his words—he offers a public bath or baptism. John's baptism is a baptism that, when

36

received with repentance, both does something and shows something: what his baptism *does* is cleanse people spiritually so that they can meet the incoming kingdom of God; what his baptism *shows* is that one means with one's whole physical life what one believes with one's heart.

John the Baptist comes on like the last great prophet of the Old Testament, like a walking, breathing law of God, full of doom and holiness and ultimacy. He is in the front of our New Testament four times in order to put the law of God in front of us four times, just before Jesus comes to us four times with gospel. John is the law of God in person; Jesus is the gospel of God in person.

John the Baptist's essential message in the third chapter of Matthew is that the will of God is to be done by the people of God or else we too will perish in the coming wrath of God, especially if we claim to be serious people of God. (In Matthew, John's message is addressed first of all to separatist Pharisees and to the sophisticated establishmentarian Sadducees, 3:7. Since each of us leans in either the separatist or the sophisticated direction, each of us is addressed by John's sermon today.)

Listen to John speak to us:

So bear the fruit [that is, live the life] that is worthy of a completely changed life. And [John continues] don't you dare say to yourselves that "We have [a substitute in] Father Abraham," because I tell you, God is able to create children for

Abraham out of these stones here. No, the ax is already resting at the root of the trees, ready to strike, and every tree that is not producing good fruit [living the just life] is chopped off and thrown into the fire (Matt. 3:8-10).

John the Baptist perpetually reminds people who begin their New Testaments that God wants the just life or else. John the Baptist's message of law is the message of the indispensability of the life of spiritual and social righteousness. John the Baptist is not at the beginning of our gospels in order to be replaced later by Jesus of Nazareth, any more than the law of God is in our Bibles in order to be replaced by the gospel (Matt. 5:17; Rom. 3:31). John is at the beginning of our gospels in order to make the people of God hungry for the righteousness, the social justice, and the moral life that only Jesus of Nazareth can fully inspire and impute. Jesus gives the power to live at the spiritual level and in the social width that John requires. John points to the heights; Jesus lifts us to them. John tells us where to go; Jesus takes us there. John the Baptist scares hell out of us; Jesus places heaven and its humanity within us. John preaches the law in its rugged majesty; Jesus brings the gospel in its empowering fullness.

John the Baptist's message of judgment is largely missing in contemporary preaching. One fruit of this craven skipping of the judgment that is on every other page of Scripture is a dull gospel. What urgent need for salvation do people have when their lives are in no great danger; when, as we hear, "God is love, and we are accepted as we are"? Honestly teaching the texts about John the Baptist will restore the needed message of God's judgment to our churches.

John's sermon concludes by telling how the coming Messiah will, by a baptism, give the power to live in the will of God.

> *I* simply baptize you with water into a changed life. But the one who is coming after me is so much stronger than I am; I am not even worthy to carry his sandals. *He* will baptize you with the Holy Spirit and fire. His winnowing fork is in his hand, and he will completely cleanse his threshing floor, and he will gather his wheat into his barn, but the chaff he will burn with a fire that never goes out (Matt. 3:11-12).

The greatest contribution of John the Baptist to the Bible was that he not only preached law, he promised gospel; he not only preached judgment, he preached Christ's Baptism with the Spirit. John the Baptist is the perfect bridge between the Testaments. He summarized the Old Testament law (and gospel) in power, and he set up the New Testament (law and) gospel in grace. John not only threatened, he provided. The enduring achievement of John the Baptist in connection with the doctrine of the Spirit is John's making the gift of the Holy Spirit an exclusively Christocentric gift: "I baptize you with water; *he* will baptize you with the Holy Spirit." John (the law) cannot give the Spirit. Only the gospel (Jesus) can—by a unique Baptism.

John the Baptist tied the coming baptism in the Holy

Spirit and fire exclusively to the coming Christ. John was a good preacher: he preached God's high law and God's insistence on the fruitful life, and then John preached God's gracious gospel, where the Messiah comes down and does something life-transforming to us. Good preachers to this day follow the pattern set by John the Baptist: they preach both law and gospel, both high moral-social demands and deep spiritual-social resources. They warn believers of God's judgment on careless life, and they promise believers that they will be overwhelmed by the power that Christ's Spirit brings; they make us want to be real, and, through preaching the gospel, they promise us Christ's Spirit to enable us to be real.

Jesus, like John, came with both law and gospel, with both fire and Spirit, with both hard words and gentle ones, with both judgment and salvation (cf., e.g., Luke 6:20-26; Matt. 5:3-12; 23:13-29; 11:20-24, 25-30). He embraced people who were struggling, exhausted, and in need of rest, and he excoriated towns where he had done many miracles but where lives had not been changed (Matthew 11).

But we are unfaithful to the witness of the New Testament and the grace of John's sermon if we do not also stress that the *major* gift Jesus came bringing was, as John the Baptist predicted, the gift of an overwhelming Spirit, the gift of an inundation or Baptism with a fiery Holy Spirit. Chrysostom, in his late fourth-century homily on this text in Matthew, calls this baptismal gift "the Mystery," by which he means that Christ's Spirit-

40

baptism by fire is nothing less than Christ's own coming, through Baptism, to dwell in our hearts by his Spirit (Col. 1:26-27; Eph. 1:9-10; 3:9). Chrysostom asks, pointedly, why did John the Baptist not predict the coming Messiah's miracles or teaching, or (we may ask) his passion or resurrection? Why did the Baptist stress only the mystery of Christ's coming with the Spirit in *Baptism* instead of stressing Christ's many other ministries? This is Chrysostom's provocative answer: "Because this [mystery of the indwelling Spirit] was greater than all [the other things that Jesus came to do], and for its sake all those [other miracles] were done." [1] The mystery is that when the Messiah comes, as Chrysostom points out beautifully, the Messiah is not predicted as just "giving" us the Holy Spirit, he is predicted as "baptizing" us with the Holy Spirit; that is, the coming Christ will lavish the Holy Spirit on us, grant the Spirit to us in unimaginable fullness. John's baptism can get us wet and turn our lives around; but Jesus' Baptism can give us internal power and fire us with the energy we need to keep our lives in perpetual repentance. (The first of Luther's 95 Theses has these unforgettable words which summarize exactly what Jesus' Spirit-Baptism came to enable: "When our Lord and Master Jesus Christ said 'Repent,' he intended for the whole life of believers to be one of repentance.")

John the Baptist's promise has come true. Jesus came as the Messiah and converted people to himself by giving them his fiery gift. I do not believe that we instruct the people of God often enough in all that we have already been given in our Christian Baptisms. Many Christian people are looking for a power they already have; we are searching for something that God has already placed within us. Faithful preaching will encourage searching Christians to accept by faith what Jesus has already given us in Baptism.

In Baptism we were given the Holy Spirit. As the people of God, we do not have to be given special spiritual conditions or new, startling demands in order to have the power we need to live our lives patiently or victoriously; we only need to believe the gospel that tells us that when we were baptized we were given the gift of the Spirit. We do not need to speak in tongues or to have other spiritual gifts or external evidence before we can be assured that we have the Spirit in fullness in our lives. All we need is faith in Christ (Luther's *Glaubst du, so hast du*).

In the all-important matter of the Spirit's presence, there is nothing that searching Christian people have to do at all; there is no looking ahead to certain steps to be taken; there is simply the looking back with faith at the gifts already given in an unprepossessing Baptism. We have all the resources we need for overcoming the evil one, for resisting temptation, for being adequate in our callings, for living the moral life, for courage in failure, and for seeking justice and peace in ways of wisdom. For the Holy Spirit was placed within us at our Baptism, and faith—simple faith in Christ, the faith that sighs and says its prayers—receives the power of the indwelling Holy Spirit again and again. (For the Christian, there are as many fillings with the Spirit as there are prayers.) Gospel preaching and the faithful administration of the sacraments encourage this faith into life again and again. The Christian ministry exists, among other reasons, to preach to the people of God the privileges that our ours in Christ—purchased for us at the cross, validated at the resurrection, delivered to us in Baptism, activated in us again and again when we believe the good news delivered to us in sermons and sacraments, and finally fully, thrillingly ours without any more struggle in the glorious return of Christ. Christian preaching, Baptism, and the Lord's Supper seek to present God's deeds in Christ (past, present, and future) in such a way that the people of God will *believe* again; and when we truly believe, we change, we repent.

Preaching, Baptism, and the Lord's Supper, along with fellowship and prayer, are the evangelical-catholic delivery systems that communicate the benefits of Jesus' cross and resurrection to us. Faith is the tap that opens us to the enjoyment of the benefits delivered to us in sermon and sacrament, fellowship and prayer. We were given an internal fire when the water of Christian Baptism touched us, and the people of God want to know this.

"Then Jesus arrived from Galilee at the Jordan River to be baptized by John" (Matt. 3:13). The first thing we must allow ourselves to do is to be surprised that Jesus got baptized at all. For John preached the coming Christ as a baptizer, not a recipient of baptism. John had said that the Christ would come baptizing his people with Holy Spirit and fire, not that he would come with sinners and have *himself* baptized in *water*. But here Jesus, in his own baptism, permanently unites water with the Spirit as the concrete locus of the church's one Baptism. Baptism is where the Spirit is given to both the Messiah now and to the people of God later (Matt. 28:19). Jesus inaugurates Christian Baptism in water as the place where the people of God receive the Baptism with the Spirit. Disciples are not above their Lord. Where he received the Spirit is where we receive the Spirit: in Baptism, in water.[2]

The surprise in our text is that John had preached the Christ as one who brings ax, winnowing fork, and fire, not as a seeker in a mass evangelistic meeting. Imagine, for example, that I am holding evangelistic meetings by Lake Michigan, and I announce that Dr. Billy Graham will be coming soon to preach, that I am not worthy to carry his briefcase behind him, that while I preach from notes, he will preach extempore, that while I am lucky to get one convert an evening, he gets thousands. And then one night Dr. Graham does arrive, but it is not on the platform, it is beneath it at the penitents' bench during the invitation. That is what is happening here. John preaches the Messiah, and he arrives—with the sinners, to *be* baptized, and not yet to give his baptism.

This is the first recorded adult act of Jesus in the gospel of Matthew, and I like to consider it Jesus' first miracle: the miracle of his humility. It is well known that Jesus ends his career on a cross between two thieves; it is not as well known that Jesus began his public career in a river amid penitent sinners. Jesus first goes down into the deep waters with his people, completely identifying *with* them, and only then does he come up and begin his ministry *to* them. In this identifying baptism of Jesus can be found a whole theology of the relation of minister to people, as well as theologies of lay ministry, of mission, of social work, and of evangelism. First Jesus was with his people in deep waters, and *then* he ministered to them in deep teaching and touching.

After John had tried unsuccessfully to dissuade Jesus from being baptized (Matt. 3:14-15), we read the final verses and the most important words in the entire chapter:

> And when Jesus had been baptized, immediately he came up from the water; and look, the heavens were opened to him, and he saw the Spirit of God coming down like a dove right toward him, and look, a voice speaking from the heavens, saying, "This is my priceless Son; I am deeply pleased with him" (Matt. 3:16-17).

Three great things happen to Jesus (the heavens open; the Spirit descends; the Father speaks), two of them singled out by Matthew's punctuating word *look*. First, "look," the dove-Spirit descends from the newly opened heavens and comes right to Jesus; and second, "look," the Father's voice announces Jesus as his priceless servant-Son (Isaiah 42; Psalm 2). These two gifts (of the Spirit and of the Father) tell us the two main things we need to know about the accreditation of Jesus. They also tell the future church the two main gifts given to it by and with Jesus in the baptism that he formally delivers to it at the end of the gospel (see the Father, Son, and Spirit *in action* here in the baptism of 3:16-17 and again *in one name* in the baptism of 28:19).

The gospel narratives do not serve primarily biographical interests (not even in Matthew, *contra* Strecker); they are recorded primarily to elicit faith and to build up the church. Thus the story of the baptism of Jesus at the beginning of the gospel is not intended to teach the church only what happened once to Jesus at his baptism a long time ago. Nor is Jesus' Last Supper at the end of the gospel simply biographical information in Jesus' interesting *vita*. Rather, Jesus inaugurates the church's Baptism by means of his own ministry— just as he inaugurates the church's Communion by means of his ministry-summarizing last meal. Both of the dominical sacraments are anchored in, and inaugurated by, Jesus' own ministry.

Thus, triune Baptism happens first in the person of its inagurator, Jesus, and Matthew intends this trinitarian baptismal fact to be seen and heard by all who read and hear his gospel from beginning (3:16-17) to end (28:19). Everything Jesus did was in the service of his people; this service begins at least as early as his baptism. One way Jesus' baptism serves us is by teaching us exactly what happens to us when we are baptized

46

in him. For the two great things that happened to him are directly related to the two great things that happen to us: through him we too are given the gift of the Spirit, and we too are given the voice of the Father's love. Let us look at these two gifts in particular.

First, the baptized are given the gift of the dove-Spirit. The form of the Spirit is revealing. The Spirit did not come down as a tiger or an eagle. Just as Jesus completely redefined what being a Messiah was by being baptized *with* people before he gave Baptism *to* them, by going down in the waters with sinners before he began his ministry of lordship over them, so also when the Holy Spirit came down as a dove almost everything anyone had ever thought about the work of the Spirit before was redefined and finessed. The dove has been the biblical symbol of creation and re-creation ever since Gen. 1:2, of peace ever since Noah (Genesis 8), and of gentleness and innocence ever since Jesus' sermon on mission (Matt. 10:16): "Be as wise as serpents and innocent as doves." When Jesus and his people are given the dove-Spirit, therefore, they do not immediately become great balls of fire or apocalyptic marvels; but they do become *gentle*men and *gentle*women, recreated by the Spirit, as the Gospels, Epistles, and experience show. The same Spirit who was the source of the quiet power of the ministry of Jesus in the Gospels empowers us in our mission.

Fluttering in the breast of every baptized person is the gentle Spirit, and, as we believe in Jesus Christ, the Spirit is at work in quiet power in our lives, conform-

47

ing us to Christ and sending us out into the world in quiet service. It is no little gift that the people of God are given the presence of God inside their psychic lives in the person of the very Spirit of God. Two spirits live inside every Christian: one's own spirit and the Spirit of the living God. This means that we have *all* the resources we need for living the Christian life fruitfully and for faithfully performing the Christian mission God assigns to each of us.

There are two exclamations or "looks!" in the account of Jesus' baptism, the "look" that accents the Spirit's descent and the "look" that introduces the Father's voice of assurance. The second gift of Baptism to believers is the voice of assurance that says, "This is my priceless Son, I am deeply pleased with him." In Jesus' case, this voice is an assurance of what Jesus already is; in the case of all the rest of us, this is the voice of adoption, regenerating us into children of God and forgiving us our sins.[3] This voice of assurance can be called the objective gift, which sets us in a relation of favor with the heavenly Father, just as the gift of the Holy Spirit is the subjective gift, which empowers us from within.

The important thing for believers to know and for the church to preach with all possible vigor is that we receive *two* great gifts in Baptism: the Holy Spirit within and a right relation with God without, that is, the Spirit and the forgiveness of sins, power and grace. For example, when Peter's Pentecost sermon hit home and the hearers were pricked in their hearts and asked, "Brethren, what shall we do?" Peter's paradigmatic reply was: "Repent, and be baptized every one of you in the name of Jesus Christ for [1] the forgiveness of your sins; and [2] you shall receive the gift of the Holy Spirit" (Acts 2:37-39 RSV). Baptism cleanses us from our sins and it empowers us with the Spirit; it removes the past from our back and it gives us power for the future; it sets us in a right relation with God and it sends us out in the world with energy for mission. The people of God need to know that we have been given these two great gifts so that we can live in their power. Recently, a thoughtful woman wrote me a letter in which she discussed the Pentecostal emphasis on the Holy Spirit. She concluded her letter this way, and I prize her words:

> It disturbed me that if we receive the Holy Spirit at baptism, why do the Pentecostals seem to have so much more "life" and maybe even "power" than most of us? Could this mean they are right? My conclusion is that these Christians *know* they have the Holy Spirit. They aren't sitting around wondering whether or not they have received it. Could it be that what we in mainline reformed churches need to do is *believe* that we received the Holy Spirit at baptism, know he is with us and thus begin to move in faith? I believe this is true![4]

I believe this is true, too. We were given the gift of the Spirit and the gift of forgiven lives in Baptism, and we do not need to do any good work, even the good work of a hyped-up faith, in order to get what we think we lack. God gave us forgiveness and the Spirit freely in Baptism, and simply being told what God has already given us will help the people of God to believe and so live in power and patience. (The similarity between the church's gift of Baptism in the New Testament and ancient Israel's gift of the land in the Old Testament is striking. Israel's big problem in the early period of its life through the period of Joshua and the Judges was believing that God really had given it the land. One of our big problems in the period of the church is believing that we are already gifted people. One thinks of the beautiful ascription in the epistle to the Ephesians: "Now to him who by the power at work within us is able to do far more abundantly than all that we ask or think, . . ." (Eph. 3:20-21 RSV).

The 16th-century Reformation rediscovered the exquisite joy of being completely forgiven, and it passed this joy on to us. The heirs of this Reformation have been teaching this great contribution to the whole church catholic to this day. One cannot read a page of Luther without feeling the forgiveness of sins. Reading Luther makes me chuckle internally, no matter how serious his subject matter, because as I read him I feel the good news of being a completely covered human being who, for the sake only of Jesus Christ's perfect righteousness, is accepted by God as a good person, pleasing in his sight. All my internal problems and spiritual and social failures are covered and forgiven because of the wonderful sacrifice of Jesus Christ given to me, along with faith, by the gift of the Holy Spirit.

The Reformation recovered the apostolic treasures of grace; it gave us the glory of the objective.

But the Reformation was burned by the subjectivist *Schwaermer* or fanatics, the "crazy saints," who, as Luther put it, swallowed the Holy Spirit feathers and all, and who introduced myriad legalisms into the church under the cover of the Spirit. Reading Luther's treatise "Against the Heavenly Prophets" (1525) is like reading accounts of some contemporary Pentecostal and charismatic Christianities. The legalism of spiritualism is a historical fact, from first-century Corinthianism or second-century Montanism to our charismatic and evangelical present. Is there anything in Christendom as horrible as meeting someone who parades as one filled with the Spirit? It is the modern abomination of desolation. The problem that has accompanied the appreciation of the Spirit has been the theology of glory. Emphasis on the forgiveness of sins is the great contribution of the Lutheran theology of the cross. Is it possible for us to have, *at the same time,* forgiveness's theology of the cross and the Spirit's theology of glory? This is a question that the two gifts of Baptism force us to ask, and it is not an easy question to answer.

The story of Jesus' baptism and the texts of Acts and the Epistles teach us clearly that Christians are given two great gifts in Baptism: the adopting forgiveness of sins and the empowering gift of the Holy Spirit, the objective and the subjective, grace and power, remission and mission, the presence of the cross and the presence of the resurrection. Why, then, has the Christian church been able to accommodate successfully only one of the two, only half of the whole, only (in sober churches) the theology of the cross and forgiveness but not at the same time the theology of glory and the Spirit? (Churches that emphasize a theology of glory and Spirit have been historically either relatively moribund or offensively fanatical.) Can we have both theologies at the same time—of the cross and of glory—without the aridity of cold orthodoxy on the one hand or the asininity of hot charismaticism on the other?

Let me broach an answer to this urgent question here at the end of this lecture in the form of a brief exegesis of a text I have already referred to in Acts. I believe ← that congregations living or even approximating the program announced in Acts 2:42 are congregations living at once in both the humility of Jesus' theology of the cross and in the missionary power of the Spirit's theology of glory. Acts 2:42 presents to us a church with a quartet of ministries—ministries of the Word, of fellowship, of sacraments, and of prayer. The text says, "And they continued steadfastly in the apostles' teaching and fellowship, in the breaking of bread and the prayers." Where these four apostolic ministries are given priority, there we are in a church that lives, a balanced church, a church that is not so centered on the cross that we forget that there was and is a resurrection and a Holy Spirit, but a church that is not so centered on the resurrection and the Spirit that it forgets that the Lord has wounds and that the Spirit is a dove, not a hawk.

52

First, the church in Acts "continued steadfastly in the apostles' teaching." This happens today in a regular program of disciplined evangelical, expository preaching and teaching, where pastors and teachers make themselves liege-servants of an absolutely honest exegesis of the successive paragraphs of Scripture, especially in the Gospels. Evangelical expository preaching is the "continuing steadfastly in the apostles' teaching" that points churches in the right direction. Such preaching gives churches the dimension of depth.

Second, the koinonia groups that meet for internal fellowship and often for external service are the "fellowship" of which Acts 2:42 speaks. Some fellowship is almost purely internal, mutual, for those within the group. This is a legitimate form of Christian fellowship. Some Christians serve so extensively in the world or church that they need the refreshment of simple, unpractical, nondirected conversation and camaraderie with mutual friends. On the other hand, some fellowship, like an Amnesty International group, for example, is organized outwardly in service to others. This form of fellowship has a long and distinguished pedigree in the history of the church (one thinks of the great voluntary movements, many of which sprang out of the 19th-century church) and is another legitimate expression of koinonia. Koinonia of both types—internal and external, support and service — gives the church the dimension of width.

The primal dimension of depth—the apostles' teaching—and the corollary dimension of width—fellowship

—are linked by an "and" in our text. This indicates that the two go together, that koinonia-fellowship is a natural spin-off from the apostolic teaching preceding and inspiring it. It is a simple observation of experience that spiritually sensitive sermons everywhere create the fellowship of Bible study and that socially sensitive sermons inevitably spawn the fellowship of outreach and service groups. Evangelical expository preaching, happily, requires faithful Christian ministry to be both spiritual and social because Scripture is everywhere both spiritual and social. (In the New Testament, for example, one thinks of the very social Synoptics and of the very spiritual John and Paul, or in the Old Testament, of the very social prophets and of the very spiritual Psalms; one thinks especially of our Lord, at once entirely human and entirely divine.) The God-given fruit of evangelical expository preaching will be churches that have spiritual support groups *and* social outreach groups, according to the varied distribution of gifts.

The next pair of ministries is "the breaking of bread and the prayers," coupled also with a linking "and," indicating by the "and" that the Lord's Supper and prayer meetings are in something like a symbiotic relationship and are nourished by each other's presence. "Breaking of bread" is simply the frequent and serious participation in the Lord's Supper; it is this sacramental seriousness that gives churches the worshipful dimension, the dimension of height, a dimension deeply needed in a world awash in mechanical-technical cacophony.

Prayer meetings, finally, are probably the least frequent kinds of meetings in churches, but without them our churches languish. (How many more committee meetings do we have than prayer meetings? What this comparison tells us is that we do not always believe in God.) In paragraph after paragraph in the gospel, Jesus tells his disciples that "this kind does not come out except by prayer" (Mark 9:29), or "Ask, and you shall receive, seek, and you shall find, knock and there will be openings. Because everyone who asks gets, and the person who seeks finds, and knockers get openings" (Matt. 7:7-8). Prayer is one of Jesus' best and most emphasized gifts according to the gospels, and a nonpraying congregation is like a nonbreathing person: enroute to death. Prayer is the breathing dimension of length or extension.

It is important to notice in Acts 2:42 that all four of these ministries—teaching, fellowship, sacrament, and prayer — occur *together* in the earliest church. The church continued steadfastly in all four dimensions— depth, width, height, and length—together. The best fellowship is, in fact, that which circles around the teaching of Scripture, and prayer meetings flourish most when they are surrounded by biblical teaching on the one side and the Lord's Supper on the other. Having the sacrament almost as often as we have teaching adds the dimension of height to the dimension of depth, and asking how we can share our gifts with the people who are hurting in our parish, community, and larger world gives the church the always-needed dimension of width. But social programs without worship services soon wither and die, and worship without the services of social justice is anathematized in Scripture (c.f., e.g., Amos 5). All four dimensions—scriptural depth, social width, eucharistic height, and prayerful length—need each other in order to be balanced, alive, and legitimate.

Thus the Holy Spirit is given to the church through the means of grace: through preaching (e.g., Acts 2:14-36 and *passim*), through Baptism (Acts 2:38-39 and *passim*), and then again and again through continuing apostolic teaching, koinonia, eucharist, and prayer (Acts 2:42 and *passim;* 1 Corinthians 12, and especially 1 Cor. 12:13).

I do not believe that God would have given the gift of the Holy Spirit and such rich means for receiving this gift if it would have been bad for the church to have the Holy Spirit. But we have been burned so often in the history of the church by triumphalist spirits that we sometimes wonder about God's wisdom. Is it really possible, we can legitimately ask, for members of the church to believe that they are filled with the Holy Spirit without their getting a big head and becoming impossible? Regular biblical teaching pricks fanatical presumptions; regular koinonia gives wholesome outlets and corrective counsel for the varied spiritual gifts; regular Holy Communion humbles the church with the holiness of God; regular prayer meetings teach believers to look outside themselves for help. Congregations that approximate the balanced quadrilateral life of Acts 2:42 are congregations experiencing both the reforming theology of the cross and the renewing theology of the glory of the Spirit—when and where it pleases God, as we must always add to avoid spiritual technology.

When you and I were baptized into the name of the Father and the Son and the Holy Spirit, we were given to the Triune God and that God was given to us. We were given the Father, above us in love and beneath us with everlasting arms in forgiveness. We were given the Son beside us; we were given the gift of the Spirit within us. We are covered on all sides—above, beneath, beside, and within. We have all that we need to be fruitful Christians in the world, fruitful in quite different ways, depending on our gifts, but fruitful in some way.

There is a great wide world out there needing the forgiveness and majesty of the Creator God, the solidarity and body of the Son, and the power and fellowship of the Spirit. We have the Word and the sacraments, the koinonia and the prayer, by which the Father has given fellowship to us and to the world. We are very, very privileged people, and this privilege translates immediately into the responsibility of mission—of many different kinds of mission. For some of us it may be evangelistic; for others, it may be social mission here and abroad; and perhaps for most pastors, it will be a mission of faithful expository preaching and teaching to the people of God in this and other countries.

The *message* we proclaim, when it is biblical exposition centering in Christ, and when God chooses to bless it, really brings the Holy Spirit and spiritual quickening, as we have all experienced in living congregations. The *sacraments* we administer actually give people the fresh sense of the forgiveness of sins and the renewed gift and gifts of the Spirit, as all Christian history joyfully confesses.

We are the ministry of God. We should so center our work on Christocentric preaching, trinitarian Baptism, apostolic teaching, social service, sacramental worship, and evangelical prayer meetings that our parishes will be filled with the Holy Spirit and moved by the challenge of world mission. We expect that Jesus Christ is coming one more time, perhaps soon, with judgment and with grace, with (as it were) one last Baptism in the Holy Spirit and fire. When he comes, he will separate sheep from goats and good shepherds from evil shepherds. The unbelieving and careless shepherds will be held responsible for the death of the sheep, and the believing and careful shepherds will be rewarded with abundant consolation (Ezekiel 34). So let us believe the gospel, feed his sheep with evangelical exposition, and tend his flock with sacramental prayer and fellowship, in the grace of the Lord Jesus Christ, with the love of God, and by the power of the Holy Spirit.

Note on the gifts of the Spirit

I would not be teaching the New Testament doctrine of the Holy Spirit with requisite fullness if I failed to mention the doctrine of the gifts of the Spirit. Let me therefore append this discussion of gifts.

Paul's theology of the charismatic gifts of the Spirit specifically teaches us that the Spirit comes in different sizes, shapes, or functions in every believer. The gift of the Spirit is not standardized or uniform; in every individual believer the Spirit takes on a unique, specific form, equipping each of the faithful with a special ministry. The First Letter of Peter helpfully divides Paul's variously numbered gifts into two main types—gifts of speaking and gifts of service—like this:

As each [of you] has received a gift, employ it for one another, as good stewards of God's many-colored grace: when any of you speaks, speak as one who utters oracles of God; when any of you renders service, do it as one who renders it by the strength that God supplies (1 Peter 4:10-11).

Not all of us are gifted as speakers and not all of us are gifted as social servants, but each of us is usually more one than the other. We are to discover who we are and be that. The curse of Christian life is trying to be someone we are not, with gifts we do not have.

I had two horrendous experiences in my own life in connection with spiritual gifts: once when I tried to be an evangelist, and once when I tried to be a social worker. Telling these stories may illustrate negatively how *not* to be misled in the matter of the gifts of the Spirit.

Bill Bright began the work of Campus Crusade for Christ in my home congregation, the First Presbyterian Church of Hollywood, California, and I was some of Bill's earliest cannon fodder. I was very timid, even cowardly, in talking to other people about faith in Christ. Bill was very effective. He told us a verse in the book of Proverbs, "The fear of man is a snare" (29:25), and he warned that Jesus himself had said that "every tree that does not bear fruit will be cut down and thrown into the fire" (Matt. 7:19). Bearing fruit, we were told, was winning other men and women to faith in Christ. If this was what fruit was, then I was ripe for the fire, because I was consistently nervous in almost every conversation about Christian faith that I had with fellow students at Occidental College.

I remember vividly that one Sunday night as I was about to enter the wonderful, lively College Department meeting at the First Presbyterian Church of Hollywood for another evening of inspiration, singing, and message, I suddenly resolved, "No, I'm not going to go in there one more time before I finally win one other person to faith in Christ." I remembered Bill Bright telling me that he had never found others hostile when he had talked to them about their spiritual lives. So I walked down to Hollywood Boulevard and Gower Street. There was a marine sitting on the bench waiting for the bus. A young woman I knew from the church, Barbara, was standing a few feet away. I asked Barbara to pray for me because I was going to speak to the marine about faith in Christ. I sat down next to the marine and said, "Excuse me, but have you ever thought about Jesus Christ?" And the marine said to me, "If you don't get out of here in 10 seconds I am going to punch you right in the teeth."

60

My father had taught me never to run away from a fight, but I thought that this situation was ridiculous, so I left as gracefully as one can under such conditions. As I hurried down the street I thought to myself, "The Lord is testing me to see if I have the courage to go on after this initial discouragement. Besides, I came on with that marine too fast. I've got to approach strangers more gradually." So I walked down the other side of Hollywood Boulevard quite a ways (out of sight of the marine!) until I came to another bus stop. There I started up a normal conversation with another gentleman. Then the bus came and took him away. That was my first great evangelistic journey.

I could tell you of other disastrous missionary attempts: with my own parents once, a couple of experiences at Princeton University that were very awkward, and others. I was not really delivered from this demon of trying to be what I was not until I attended a chapel service at Princeton Theological Seminary where Eugene Carson Blake read from 1 Cor. 12:4ff. these words: "Now there are varieties of gifts, but the same Spirit; and there are varieties of service, but the same Lord; and there are varieties of working, but it is the same God who inspires them all in every one. To each is given [a particular expression] of the Spirit for the common good." Then and there I resolved to stop trying to be like the Christian evangelists I admired so much and to become a student instead, the very thing I found myself longing to be. I had no assurance that there was much that a student could do for the world missionary enterprise, but I knew that I loved reading, and I hoped that somehow being a student (and perhaps, therefore, a teacher) could lead others to find Christ.

Bill Bright really does have the gift of evangelism; I have seen it myself. But my mistake was in thinking that I, too, must have this gift or else I was a second-class, fruitless Christian. It is really very foolish of us when we try to be someone we admire rather than to be who we are.

There is a person inside each one of us that the uniquely shaped gift of the Holy Spirit is trying to bring into being. Thank God for the evangelists of the world. Without them, we church teachers would not have anyone to teach, and many preachers would be without congregations. We greatly need those who have the boldness of the Spirit to talk freely with people about faith in Christ. But talking to individuals is not everyone's gift, though at times it is certainly everyone's responsibility.

The other time that I went off in a questionable spiritual direction was when my wife and I were United Presbyterian missionaries in the Philippines. After our first term of five years at Union Theological Seminary outside Manila, Kathy and I decided that it would be wise for us to live and work in a Philippine town for the first year of our second five-year term, and we prepared to do that. The main spiritual reason for our wanting to do this was that we were shamed again and again by talks in the seminary chapel and at church about the great need of people out in the real world and about the shallowness of our merely teaching people with words in the safe confines of the seminary. What the world needed, we were told repeatedly, was servants, not talkers; deeds, not words; doers, not teachers—out in the real world, not inside seminaries. So we prepared to launch out. I will not tell you all the details of our misadventure because they are too embarrassing and shaming to Kathy, me, and the dear people we were supposed to serve. Just let me say this: we soon beat a hasty retreat back to the seminary because we were not able to live in the town where we were assigned. I am not proud of that incident in our lives; it was probably the most painful episode in our Christian career. But I have wondered since: Why did Kathy and I have such weak egos, such personal insecurity, that we did not believe that our teaching ministry was good enough? Why did we believe that unless we stopped being teachers we could not *really* be missionary disciples? I have come to the conclusion that I am a pushover for authority. When I was a young Christian, I was deeply impressed by those who won others to Christ in strong ministries of evangelism; when I began work as a missionary, I was deeply impressed by those who had strong ministries of social service. I still believe that those who have the spiritual ministry of evangelism and the social ministry of service are doing the nitty-gritty, hand-to-hand combat in the army of God that is the most basic work in the kingdom. I am convinced that in some ways as a teacher I am behind the battle lines where the church engages the world in all its raw power. But even the infantry has to eat, and soldiers have to come to the rear to the mess hall at least occasionally. There is a place for us who teach, though it is a modest place. Evangelists, social workers, and preachers are out at the front and will get their special rewards; but we who live with books have a place, too. The educational apostolate can stand alongside the social, evangelistic, and pastoral apostolates with a good conscience; we are all parts of the body of Christ, and we all need each other. The key thing is for each of us to be who each of us is, for us to love and pray for the other parts of the body of Christ, to serve the others and let them serve us, and meanwhile to let no one rob us of our own gift and function, however odd or even substandard it may seem to others to be (1 Cor. 12:4-31; Luke 10:38-42).

Each of us receives the Holy Spirit in the shape of a particular charisma in Holy Baptism. The gift is activated in us effectively when we believe the Lord and seek ways of serving him. One of the most exciting things in life is to find what God is trying to make us be and then literally to shape up.

3 The Theology of the Cross and the Holy Spirit

William Hordern

Central to Martin Luther's thinking was the theology of the cross. This is not to say that the theology of the cross is in any way a uniquely Lutheran doctrine. One of the best modern books on the subject comes from the Reformed theologian, Jurgen Moltmann, in his book *The Crucified God*. It is my conviction that a theology of the cross is crucial for the church today. On all sides we are surrounded by what Luther would have called a "theology of glory." Because of this, there is an urgent need for the church to recapture the truth of the theology of the cross. Therefore, in these lectures I have decided to look at the Holy Spirit in light of a theology of the cross.

First, it should be made clear that a theology of the cross is not among the many doctrines that make up Christian belief. Rather, it is a way of looking at and understanding *all* doctrines. When I speak of looking at the Holy Spirit in the light of the theology of the cross, I am not looking at two different doctrines. I am looking at the doctrine of the Holy Spirit, but I am looking at it through the framework of a theology of the cross.

Luther developed his theology of the cross over against the dominant spirit of the church of his day which he called a theology of glory. In many ways that is an unfortunate term to describe the phenomena in question. After all, in Christian circles "glory" is usually a good word. I have found that when I have lectured to groups on the contrast of a theology of the cross and a theology of glory, many people leap to the conclusion that what we need is a proper balance between the two, since both cross and glory are important aspects of Christianity. But this misses the whole point; we are not here dealing with a both/and, but with an either/or.

Personally, I have come to prefer the use of the term *triumphalism* to describe the opposite of a theology of the cross. Triumphalism describes what seems to be the normal human approach to religion. The natural person turns to religion to receive victories and triumphs from the divine beings. Health, wealth, and good fortune are hence seen as evidence that one has gained the favor of the gods and goddesses. The divine is found in the outstanding, the out-of-the-ordinary, the ecstatic, and the impressive. Triumphalism leads a person to make extravagant claims about the victories brought by religious faith and practice. Luther used the term *theology of glory* because he said that the people who used this approach thought that they were already in heaven and forgot that they still were on earth. Triumphalism always forgets the limitations of being finite, sinful human beings.

There are at least four areas in which triumphalism operates. First, there is the area of knowledge. Triumphalism claims a certainty of knowledge about God and the ways of God. It is confident that, in at least some divine matters, it has the truth, the whole truth, and nothing but the truth. Hence it is prepared to cast into the outer darkness all who do not agree with it. In Luther's vivid terms, it tries to climb into heaven and pull God down to earth. From the point of view of a theology of the cross, this kind of triumphalism forgets Paul's reminder that, in this life, we always see "through a glass darkly" and "know in part" (1 Cor. 13:12 KJV). A theology of the cross does not assume that Christians abide in total ignorance, but it does know that even when and where God is revealed, God is also hidden.

Secondly, triumphalism appears in the area of sanctification. Extravagant claims are made as to the degree of moral purity that has been attained and the problems that have been overcome. Triumphalism promises that if a family prays together, it will stay together. It maintains that if one has faith, alcoholism will be overcome and psychological problems will be avoided. A theology of the cross by no means denies that Christian faith will bear fruit in a more sanctified life. But it charges that triumphalism forgets that the Christian is at one and the same time justified and sinful. It recalls that the spirit-filled church of Corinth was still faced with a host of failures in attempting to live the Christian life. John Wesley could call his followers to aim for perfection, but he avoided triumphalism by saying that perfection probably would not be achieved before one's deathbed. Reinhold Niebuhr profoundly pointed to the fallacy of triumphalist claims in the area of sanctification when he pointed out that people had to have achieved considerable ethical goodness before they were capable of commiting the worst sin—pride in their goodness.

Third, triumphalism appears in claims of victory over various forms of adversity. Triumphalism emphasizes a host of miracles and looks for miraculous cures of all ills. The triumphalistic church of Luther's time was continually telling about the latest appearance of the Virgin Mary and the miracles that followed such appearances. Multitudes of people were always on pilgrimages to various holy shrines in expectation of having their illnesses healed. Triumphalist expectations are such that those who do not experience miraculous cures are made to feel guilty, since such a failure is seen as evidence that they are lacking in faith.

A theology of the cross in no way denies the healing power of God, and where it is experienced, a theology of the cross expresses thanks. But a theology of the cross does not believe that miraculous healing is the norm for Christian life, and the lack of such miracles is not seen as a lack of faith. It recalls that Paul repeatedly prayed to be delivered from his "thorn in the flesh," but no miracle delivered him. Jesus did not promise his followers that their adversities would all be taken from them. On the contrary, he told them that following him would bring them more adversities, and hence they must be prepared to take up their crosses if they would follow him.

Most important of all, a theology of the cross repudiates triumphalism at this point by affirming that God's grace is often most evident in those Christians who are not spared adversity. God is not simply known in the person who has a miraculous cure of cancer, but even more is known in the "peace that passes understanding" which sustains the terminally ill cancer patient. It is a peace that enables one to live a Christian life in the midst of adversity, rather than a peace that comes from the removal of the adversity.

In the fourth place, triumphalism leads people to find evidence in their lives which gives the assurance of salvation. The evidence may be in the form of ecstatic or mystical religious experience. It may be in the form of improvement in one's ethical behavior and/or the overcoming of vicious habits and addictions. It may be in the form of answered prayer and/or success in business, good health, and general good fortune. When any or all of these are present, triumphalism promises that they can be seen as the assurance of God's good favor towards the person in question and assurance that they are numbered among the saved. Of course, the other side of this coin is that those who do not find these evidences in their lives are led to believe that they are in the outer darkness, living under the condemnation of God. It is obvious that triumphalism is thus most comforting to the rich, the powerful, the well-adjusted, and the successful. Triumphalism is a religion for winners with nothing much to say to losers except that, if they but had enough faith, they too could be winners.

Over against triumphalism, a theology of the cross says that we can never find assurance of our salvation by looking at ourselves. Religious experience is notoriously inconsistent. The greatest saints of the ages have known vividly the experience of the "dark night of the soul," the times when God, instead of being gloriously present to a person, seems absent. Instead of loving, God seems judgmental and even vindictive. If our experiences of God's presence and love are assurances of salvation, does it not follow that our experiences of God's absences and wrath are evidence of our rejection by God? When we look at our moral victories as evidence of our salvation, inevitably we begin to thank God that we are not as our neighbors. I recall Philip Watson shocking a group of Lutheran pastors by saying that a person could be cured of alcoholism and not be a Christian, whereas another person might be a Christian and not be cured of alcoholism. The Lutheran pastors should not have been shocked, because Watson was simply expounding Luther's theology of the cross. He was stating the implications of the Lutheran doctrine that we are saved by grace through faith and not by our works.

Turning to some of the other evidences that triumphalism finds to give assurance of salvation, it was Luther himself who declared that it is a good sign when our prayers are not answered and a bad sign when they are. Did not Paul tell us that we do not know how to pray (Rom. 8:26)? Therefore, when we do not receive that for which we prayed, it may be a better sign of God's graciousness to us than when we do receive the answer for which we prayed. As to success in business, good health, and general good fortune, we have seen before that Jesus never promised those to his followers. Hence they cannot be used as proofs that God is with us. In fact, throughout the Bible there runs the theme that the rich, the powerful, and the successful are the enemies of God, whereas the poor, the oppressed, and the defeated are of particular concern to God.

If the assurance of our salvation does not depend upon looking at ourselves, a theology of the cross affirms that it does depend upon looking at God's graciousness towards us in Jesus Christ. When Martin Luther experienced the wrath of God, when he could not believe that God could be gracious to a miserable sinner like Martin Luther, he would assure himself with the words, "I have been baptized." This was not a superstitious sacramentalism which saw Baptism as a magical rite which put a person right with God. Rather, it was Luther's way of reminding himself that his assurance never came from anything that he could find in himself; it came from what God had done for him in Christ. Baptism was the reminder that before Luther ever dreamed of looking for God, God had been looking for him. It reminded him that his place before God was not assured by any accomplishment of his, but by the gracious forgiving love which God had for him.

A theology of the cross is obviously closely related to the doctrine of justification. Triumphalism always wants to contribute something to its own salvation. Even when it talks about God's grace, it adds that we must cooperate with it, we must have faith, we need to find Christ, and so on. But a theology of the cross knows that even the faith through which we are saved comes to us as a gift. It knows that, looking at ourselves, the best we can ever say is, "I believe, help my unbelief!" (Mark 9:24).

A theology of the cross does not arise from speculation or even from an observance of the facts of the lives of Christians, although those facts do fit a theology of the cross. Paul says, "We are afflicted in every way . . ." (2 Cor. 4:8), and the lives of Christians indicate that this is true. Christians suffer from all the ills that afflict humanity. Their ethical conduct and life-styles fall far short of perfection. Those who do make triumphalist claims for themselves never appear, in the eyes of observers, to display the perfections of which they boast. Pascal made a statement that fits the lives of Christians as we see them: There are only two classes of people, the sinners who think that they are righteous and the righteous who know that they are sinners. Those Christians whose lives make the best witness to others are seldom those who make triumphalist claims for themselves, but rather those who quietly go about showing concern and love for those whom they meet, while being quite conscious of the many ways in which they fail to live the life to which Christ calls them. Nonetheless, as we have said, a theology of the cross does not depend upon these observations. From Luther on, a theology of the cross has centered in the incarnation, the revelation of God in and through the life of Jesus of Nazareth.

For Luther, the theology of the cross begins with the Christmas stories and continues on through Jesus' life to the crucifixion. Thus a theology of the cross is not based only on the crucifixion; rather, it sees the crucifixion as being the final culmination of the whole life of Christ which was lived under the cross. A theology of the cross sees that God's revelation comes in a way that refutes and disappoints human expectations. Human expectations are that the divine will be manifest in the powerful, the mighty, and the spectacular. In Jesus, however, God comes in weakness and in a hidden form. As George Macdonald put it so beautifully,

> They were looking for a king
> To slay their foes and lift them high,
> Thou cam'st a little baby thing
> That made a woman cry.

Luther was always fascinated with the Christmas story —God in the womb of a simple Jewish woman, nursed at her breast, soiling his diapers, and in all ways like any other human baby. Jesus grew both physically and in wisdom as do other children (Luke 2:52). He came from a humble carpenter's home and seems to have followed his father's trade. He had a brief ministry during which he won a considerable following for a time, but this seems to have drifted away. Finally, he was put to death in the cruel fashion that Rome reserved for runaway slaves and revolutionaries. The triumphalist has difficulty in finding in this simple life the kind of spectacular expressions of divinity that triumphalism expects.

Christians through the ages have been concerned about the hiddenness of the divine in Jesus, and thus, through the centuries, they have made much of the miracles that Jesus performed. The miracles seem the one truly divine element in a life that was otherwise lacking in the real attributes of divinity. And so Christians have used the miracle stories as proofs of Jesus' divinity. But a reading of the Gospels does not support such an apologetic.

To begin with, we need to look again at the temptations of Jesus in the wilderness. Following the account in Luke, we read that when Jesus had been in the wilderness for 40 days, the devil said to him, "If you are the Son of God, command this stone to become bread" (Luke 4:3). Here we have a typically triumphalist suggestion. If a person is truly divine, one would expect that hunger would be no problem. The divine being could be expected to provide food miraculously, if indeed food was really needed. Perhaps also involved in this temptation is the implication that food could be miraculously provided for others since, as we have seen, triumphalism looks to religion to provide a solid economic basis for life. Jesus answers, "It is written, 'Man shall not live by bread alone' " (Luke 4:4). Obviously Jesus does not say that faith has no concern with bread. We cannot use this answer, as it often has been used, to claim that Christians should be unconcerned with the problems of poverty and hunger. Jesus does not deny the importance of bread; he simply says that bread is not the only need of human beings. But obviously, in resisting this temptation to provide food miraculously, Jesus is rejecting the triumphalist view of the divine as a miracle-working provider of physical needs. Jesus is refusing to be the kind of savior triumphalism desires.

The second temptation comes by showing Jesus the kingdoms of the world and promising to give him authority over them and the glory that goes with such authority. Again we find the idea that the truly divine is best seen in power and glory. It will be manifest among the rulers, the rich, and the successful. If the Son of God appears in our midst, we should expect that he will manifest power and glory even greater than that of worldly potentates. But Jesus' answer is that Scripture calls us to worship God alone, and that means one does not take the way of worldly power and glory. This temptation seems closely related to a statement that Jesus made to his disciples later. When they were arguing as to which one of them should sit on the right hand of Jesus in the Kingdom, Jesus warned them that

although the rulers of this world lord it over their subjects, it is not to be so among his followers. True great-
ness is not found in ruling but in serving (Luke 22:24-
27). Again, Jesus resists the idea of expressing his divinity through ostentatious expressions of power and glory.

The third temptation is for Jesus to cast himself down
from the pinnacle of the temple. This is obviously a
temptation to use miracles to win followers. The sight
of a man leaping from the temple and being borne
safely to earth by angels would be a most impressive
miracle. It would certainly gain attention and doubtless
would win awe-stricken followers. But Jesus responds
by quoting the Scripture, "You shall not tempt the Lord
your God" (Luke 4:12). Jesus' answer points up the
real problem with triumphalism; it amounts to tempt-
ing God. It makes its bargain with God, saying grant
me these desires of mine, display yourself in power, and
I will believe. Jesus refuses the way of power and miraculous proof as temptations of God and offers instead
God hidden within a humble human life that can be
seen only by the eyes of faith.

But, you say, Jesus did perform miracles—is that not
a triumphalist proof of his divinity? That it was not
seems to be a point upon which both Jesus and his
enemies were agreed. The enemies claimed that Jesus
was performing the miracles by the power of Beelzebul,
the devil (Matt. 12:24). That is, at best miracles only
demonstrated the presence of unusual power, and the
power could be evil or good. The observers had to make
their own decision. Furthermore, Jesus goes on to ask

his critics, "If I cast out demons by Beelzebul, by whom do your sons cast them out?" (Matt. 12:27). This answer reveals that Jesus believed others performed similar miracles, and hence the miracle per se could not prove that the miracle worker was divine or was the Messiah.

This implication appears again in Matt. 11:2-6, when the disciples of John the Baptist come to inquire if Jesus is the expected Messiah. Jesus does not give a direct answer, but tells the disciples to return and tell John what they have seen. The blind have received sight, the lame walk, lepers are cleansed, the deaf hear, the dead are raised, and the poor are hearing good news. The triumphalist might see Jesus here using miracles to prove his messiahship. But obviously *Jesus* does not see it this way, because he goes on to say, "Blessed is he who takes no offense at me" (Matt. 11:6). In other words, Jesus does not see his miracles as proofs; at best they may force people to a decision—belief or offense. It is also interesting that, with the miracles of healing, Jesus includes the preaching of good news to the poor. For Jesus this humble act seems to have as much basis for demanding decision as the miracles.

Furthermore, it is significant that Jesus refused to perform miracles at precisely those points where they would have had the greatest power to promote belief in him. On trial before Herod, Jesus ignored Herod's desire for him to prove himself with a miracle (Luke 23:8-12). The crowd at the crucifixion called on Jesus to perform a miracle by saving himself from the cross, but he died without a miracle (Mark 15:32).

Finally, I would mention the fact that the adversaries of Jesus came and asked him for a "sign" (Mark 8:11 ff.). That is, they wanted a miracle to prove that Jesus was truly the Messiah. This request was probably sincere enough, since many were looking and hoping for the Messiah. Here was Jesus' opportunity to win these opponents by demonstrating with miracles that he was indeed their Messiah. But Jesus refused to give them such a proof.

The Gospels represent Jesus as performing miracles primarily because he had compassion for human need. He leaves people, as he left John, free to make up their own minds whether or not this reveals his messiahship. There is no evidence at all that Jesus used his miracles to prove his standing with God. On the contrary, there is evidence that he did not want to be known as a miracle worker. He repeatedly told those whom he healed to tell no one, and he often escaped from crowds that were seeking a miracle. Luther seems to have understood the Gospels when he says that the miracles were the least important of the works that Jesus performed.

Before we leave the question of whether the miracles prove the divinity of Jesus, we must look to the resurrection. Surely, it seems to many, this is a proof of Jesus' divinity. Here, at last, we have a clear triumphalist theology. But look again. The resurrection was nothing at all like the miracle the crowd asked from Jesus on the cross. If, in the public execution place, Jesus had miraculously come down from the cross, it would have been an impressive act of power that would no doubt have persuaded the doubters and probably even have moved his crucifiers to repentant worship of him. But the resurrection did not occur in public; therefore there was no one to witness the event. The risen Christ did not appear to his enemies to prove that they had been wrong, nor do we read of him appearing to the indifferent. He only appeared to his disciples and to a few of his closer followers for a brief period. Even the 500 witnesses referred to by Paul did not include the important religious leaders of the time. Most of them were too insignificant to leave their names in history. From the very beginning, then, it was quite reasonable and possible to deny the fact of the resurrection. Those who saw in Jesus' miracles the power of Beelzebul saw in the resurrection only the theft of Jesus' body from the tomb. Today, as historians wrestle with the evidence for the resurrection, they certainly can demonstrate that it is reasonable for Christians to believe that Jesus was in fact raised from the dead and did appear to his followers. But it is impossible to say that it is proven beyond all reasonable doubt. With the resurrection we are like John the Baptist's disciples. We are told the story, and then it is a case of being blessed if we do not take offense. But the choice is ours; we do not have proof.

As we read the gospel accounts of the life of Jesus, we see a truly human person, living a human life, sharing with all humanity birth and death, joy and sorrow, hunger and satisfaction, pain and pleasure. Paul must have been acutely aware of the story of Jesus' life when he wrote in Phil. 2:5ff. that Christ Jesus did not count equality with God a thing to be grasped "but emptied himself, taking the form of a servant, being born in the likeness of men . . . he humbled himself and became obedient to death. . . ." A theology of the cross sees that God has come to us in this humble human form. Contrary to human expectations, the revelation of God comes in a form that was despised and rejected precisely because Jesus did not fulfill the human expectation that God could only appear in a form of power, majesty, and supernatural awesomeness.

Because triumphalism is so natural to human expectations, it is not surprising that the first Christological heresy, docetism, denied that Jesus was fully and completely human. In various ways the docetists argued that Jesus only appeared to be human, that instead of a human soul, he had the divine logos which left his body before it suffered death on the cross. Throughout Christian history the docetic heresy has never been far from the surface of Christianity. Of course ever since the early church declared that the orthodox faith was that Jesus Christ is "very God of very God and very man of very man," Christians have been careful to pay lip service to the "real humanity" of Jesus. But in practice, Christians have continuously spoken of Jesus and portrayed him in ways that deny his real humanity.

There was an interesting illustration of this docetic tendency a few years ago when the movie *Jesus Christ*

Superstar appeared. Many Christians condemned the movie, and one of the main reasons was the way in which Jesus' temptation in Gethsemane was portrayed. Most movies that have portrayed Jesus' life have been docetic in nature. By the time such movies get to the story of Gethsemane, the viewers are so impressed with the divine nature of Jesus that they cannot take the temptation with real seriousness. This divine being, whose feet never quite seem to touch the ground, will not really be tempted. But, in *Superstar,* the Gethsemane scene portrayed a real human being torn by real temptation, seeking a way to escape the "cup" that was before him. What the critics of *Superstar* failed to see was that its portrayal was very close to what we read in the Gospels. They picture Jesus so tempted that his soul "is very sorrowful, even to death" (Matt. 26:38) and the sweat falls from him like great drops of blood (Luke 22:44). The Gospels do not picture a divine being play-acting; they portray a human person in the agony of real temptation.

Docetism arises from the fear that if Jesus is portrayed as fully human, we shall lose the doctrine of his divinity. Believing that the divine can only be found in the supernatural, triumphalism maintains that any emphasis upon the humanity and weakness of the man Jesus will result in the destruction of Christian faith that Jesus was the Christ, the second person of the Trinity. But a theology of the cross in no way denies, or wants to deny, the confession that Christ is very God of very God. It simply wants to affirm that God is most fully and completely manifest in the midst of the finiteness, humanity, and, yes, weakness of the crucified man, Jesus.

Central to Luther's development of a theology of the cross was his affirmation that the finite is capable of receiving the infinite. Luther saw no need to affirm that something must be either finite or infinite. There was no need to try to distinguish in Jesus between the finite aspects of his humanity—such as his human body, the fact that he grew tired, was hungry, and died—and the infinite aspects of his life—such as the working of miracles and rising from the dead. For Luther, the wonder of the incarnation was that God the infinite, the divine, was to be found precisely in the finite, the human. The creator was capable of being fully present in the creation. And so Luther did not hesitate to go so far as to say that, on the cross, God suffered death.

At this point, I can well imagine that some of you are wondering what I am up to. This was meant to be a discourse on the Holy Spirit, and, while I am approaching the end of my theme, I have hardly mentioned the Spirit. To date this sounds more like a discourse on Christology rather than one on pneumatology. But I disagree. I am not going to get into a discussion of the Trinity in these lectures, but suffice it to say that the doctrine of the Trinity is firmly rooted in the belief in one God. Therefore you cannot talk about one member of the Trinity without, implicitly at least, speaking about the other members. If, as I have argued, a theology of the cross is rooted in the revelation of God given to us in the incarnation, then a theology of the cross must likewise apply to God as Creator and God as Holy Spirit. There are not three gods, only the one God revealed in and through Jesus Christ.

The early church was divided by the so-called *filio-que* controversy. That is, the West added to the Nicene creed the confession that the Holy Spirit "proceeds from the Father *and the Son.*" The East refused to accept this, and Eastern and Western Christendom have traveled separate paths ever since. There has been active discussion in recent years between Rome and Orthodoxy on this issue. The whole controversy is unfortunate, inasmuch as it is based upon an attempt to draw too clearly the picture of the Trinity. But whether we say that the Spirit proceeds from Father and Son or only from the Father, all Christians have agreed that the Holy Spirit is at one with both Father and Son. If the theology of the cross is based on the incarnation, we must view the Spirit in the same light. It is interesting to find in the New Testament that the writers could speak interchangeably of the Spirit of God or the Spirit of Christ (e.g., Phil. 1:19). This alerts us to the fact that to have the Holy Spirit is to have the "mind that was in Christ"; it is to be "in Christ," to use a favorite term of Paul's. Our lengthy discussion of Christ was not meant to ignore the Holy Spirit, but rather to lay the only firm basis upon which we can understand the Holy Spirit. The New Testament warns us that we must test the spirits. There are many spirits abroad that are far from holy, and we must evaluate claims about the Spirit.

But how are we to evaluate? The only basis we have to evaluate a claim about the Spirit is the revelation that comes in Jesus Christ. If someone claims to be inspired by the Spirit and acts contrary to the spirit of Christ, we know that it is a false claim.

If, then, the theology of the cross arises from the revelation in Christ, we must apply it in understanding the Spirit. There has been a tendency among some Christians to remain faithful to a theology of the cross when speaking of Jesus. They avoid all docetism. But when they turn to the Holy Spirit, they become triumphalist. The God that was hidden even as revealed in Christ becomes purely revealed, they believe, in the experience of the Holy Spirit. When filled by the Holy Spirit, they believe that they no longer see through a glass darkly but are actually face to face with God. It was of such triumphalists that Luther said that they acted as though they had swallowed the Holy Spirit, "feathers and all."

Such triumphalists are willing to admit that God came to us in Christ in the form of weakness, hidden in a truly human life. But they see the Holy Spirit coming with a power and strength that overcomes human realities. They can sing of Christ,

How silently, how silently
The wondrous gift is giv'n!

But when it comes to the Holy Spirit, they point to the spectacular, the impressive, and anything but the silent.

In my next lecture I want to examine the Holy Spirit in the lives of Christians under the perspective of a theology of the cross. Hopefully, as I do that, the relevance of this lecture to the Holy Spirit will be apparent.

4 The Holy Spirit and the Theology of the Cross

William Hordern

To understand what it means to view the Holy Spirit in light of a theology of the cross, it will be useful if, like Luther, we contrast it with a triumphalist understanding of the Spirit and its fruits. In this lecture, therefore, I wish to look at four ways in which we frequently meet a triumphalist interpretation of the Spirit and contrast these with an interpretation in light of the theology of the cross.

First, there is that triumphalist view of the Spirit which separates the activity and presence of the Spirit from the material and the ordinary. Greek philosophy left a heritage that has greatly influenced Christian thinking over the years. It is a dualistic heritage which divides sharply between the spiritual, which is good, and matter, which is evil. People are called to cultivate a spiritual life, and this means they must deny the material life, including their own bodies. Where this presupposition is held, it is natural to look for the Holy Spirit in an inner experience of the person, because such inner experience seems to be less bodily or material than something which involves bodily actions.

In his battle with triumphalism, Luther was first concerned with the form in which it was found in the medieval Catholic church. But, as time went on, he found more and more evidences of triumphalism in the left wing forms of the Reformation itself. One of the common forms was found in the claim to be living by the direct guidance of the Holy Spirit. Those who made such claims often boasted that they did not need the written (and hence material) Word of God because God spoke directly to their hearts. They did not need to hear the preaching of other human beings. They did not need the Baptism with water, for they had the better baptism of the Spirit. They did not need the bread and wine of Communion, for they communed directly and spiritually with God in their hearts. Against such claims Luther affirmed that the God who comes to us in the human, finite form of Jesus comes to us as the Holy Spirit in the humble earthly forms of baptismal water, the bread and wine of Communion, the preaching of the Word, and the written Word of the Bible.

Today, perhaps even more than in Luther's day, there is a tendency to identify the Holy Spirit with the unusual, the ecstatic, and what is viewed as the supernatural. As one reads the literature of the neo-Pentecostals of today, we continually run across descriptions of "the great outpouring of the Holy Spirit" in our times. The evidence given for this outpouring is usually the growth of ecstatic speaking in tongues and of miracles, particularly healing miracles. In the same context certain persons are described as "Spirit-filled," and again the evidence is found in the ecstatic and unusual experiences of the individual in question. A theology of the cross in no way wishes to deny that the Holy Spirit is present and active in these unusual and ecstatic events. But it does affirm that these events, in and of themselves, are not evidence that this is a time when there is a greater outpouring of the Spirit than in other times. It also denies that such out-of-the-ordinary events and experiences are evidence that a person is more "filled with the Spirit" than other Christians who do not share the same events and experiences.

The basis for a theology of the cross's view of the Spirit is found at the very beginning of the Bible, where the Spirit is described as God's agent in creation (Gen. 1:2; 2:7). Far from being set over against the material world, the Holy Spirit was active in the creation of it. But the Old Testament never thought of creation as something that was past and finished. All existence depends upon God's continuing creation. Psalm 104 expresses this faith very well. God's creation is seen as active in the present, making the grass to grow for cattle to eat and plants to grow for human beings to cultivate. Through God's activity people have food to eat and wine to gladden their hearts. Just as in the original creation, the Spirit is seen at work also in this creative activity as we read, "When thou sendest forth thy Spirit, they are created . . ." (Ps. 104:30). The Spirit may be in the extraordinary and unusual events, but this does not make the time of such events a unique "outpouring" of the Spirit, for if God's Spirit is not being outpoured at all times, there would be no existence at all.

Sometimes Paul's sharp distinction between the flesh and the spirit is interpreted as a dualism of spirit and matter. But if there is anything that New Testament scholars agree upon, it is that this is a false interpretation. For Paul, the "flesh" described the human person living apart from God and the "spirit" represented the person living in the presence of God. Thus in Gal. 5:16-26, where Paul contrasts the works of the flesh with the works of the Spirit, nothing is based upon a body-spirit dichotomy. The first works of the flesh are listed as immorality, impurity, and licentiousness. It begins to look as if they are associated with the body, but suddenly the list changes to what the body-spirit dichotomy would have to think of as spiritual sins— idolatry, sorcery, enmity, strife, jealousy, anger, selfishness, party spirit, and envy. And then, almost as though Paul did not want to have any kind of division that relates to a separation of the physical and the spiritual, he ends with what are mainly bodily sins—"drunkenness, carousing, and the like." In short, whether something is spiritual or fleshly has nothing to do with whether or not the body and/or matter is involved. The first fruit of the Spirit, as the New Testament makes clear, is love, and love is concerned with bodily needs such as eating and drinking. Hence a cup of cold water given in Jesus' name is a spiritual act, and food given to a hungry person is a spiritual action of feeding Christ himself (Matt. 25:31-46).

When the presence of the Holy Spirit is identified with the spectacular, the unusual, and the ecstatic, many Christians are made to feel that they lack the Holy Spirit and its fullness. But this is not what the New Testament says. If people believe in Jesus Christ, that is itself evidence that they are Spirit-filled (e.g., see 1 Cor. 12:3). Christians who show loving concern for their neighbors—taking a bowl of soup to a sick person, giving a word of encouragement to a discouraged one, visiting a lonely person, and so on—are acting in the Spirit according to the New Testament.

This brings us to the next form of triumphalism with regard to the Holy Spirit. It is the tendency of some Christians to claim superiority because they have the Spirit, or more of it than others. Many Christians are made to feel inferior and guilty because they do not have in their lives the evidence of the gifts of the Spirit found in those claiming to be Spirit-filled. Obviously, this form of triumphalism is closely related to the first. Those claiming superiority are the "Spirit-filled" ones who have the more ecstatic and spectacular gifts of the Spirit.

A theology of the cross replies to such triumphalism by first affirming that the gifts of the Holy Spirit are just that—*gifts*. Paul's letters to the Corinthians are most relevant here, because the Corinthian church was filled with people taking pride in the manifestations of the Spirit in their lives. To them Paul said, "What have you that you did not receive? If then you received it, why do you boast as if it were not a gift?" (1 Cor. 4:7). John Koenig, in his study of the charismata (gifts) of the Holy Spirit, points out that the Greek word for grace *(charis)* is developed into the virtually unique New Testament use of *charisma* for gift. The gifts of the Holy Spirit thus are portrayed as being by grace and grace alone.[1] No more than salvation do the gifts of God come to those who earn or deserve them.

In 1 Corinthians 12 Paul makes a second reply to the boastful Corinthians. "Now there are varieties of gifts, but the same Spirit" (1 Cor. 12:4). Christians will not all receive the same combination of gifts, but that does not mean that one has more of the Spirit than others, for there is only one Spirit. In this context Paul lists nine different gifts of the Spirit, including the utterance of wisdom, the utterance of knowledge, healing, and speaking in tongues. Paul then presents his famous analogy of the body which consists of many members. The ear, we are told rather humorously, should not say that it is not of the body because it is not an eye. This verse should be a great comfort to ordinary Christians who do not find in their lives the more spectacular forms of gifts of which the triumphalists boast. Paul goes even further. He says that God has given "greater honor" to the inferior parts "that there may be no discord in the body" (1 Cor. 12:24-25).

Having made the point about the diversity of gifts, Paul comes to the renowned 13th chapter of 1 Corinthians which extols love. The implication is clear—the greatest gift that is received by Christians is the gift to love. In fact, without love, gifts such as speaking in tongues, prophesying, understanding, knowledge, and even faith are useless for a Christian. Furthermore, all of the other gifts will pass away, for our prophesying and our knowledge are imperfect. Hence, when the perfect comes, they will no longer be needed (1 Cor. 13:8-10). But love is forever, and a very cogent point about love is that it is not jealous or boastful (1 Cor. 13:4). This is a clear rebuke to all forms of triumphalism which would claim superiority over others on the basis of the gifts of the Spirit that have been received.

In the 14th chapter Paul tells the Corinthians to keep on seeking the spiritual gifts, but he says they should especially seek the gift of prophecy. Prophecy, he says, is speaking to human beings, whereas speaking in tongues is speaking to God, since human hearers cannot understand such speaking. In short, after love, prophecy seems the gift that should be most desired.

Given the widespread use of the word *prophecy* in our society, it is really a poor translation of what Paul is talking about. Today the term *prophet* usually means a person who can foretell the future. To illustrate, in Canada each September a group of financial analysts meet to predict the economic future of the country. A newspaper account of this year's meeting was headlined, "Prophets not so hot." It went on to tell of how wrong last year's predictions had been. One of the analysts even said, "I am not going to try to tell what went wrong with my prophecies, I am going to plead insanity." This newspaper account makes it clear that today the term *prophecy* normally means foretelling the future. But this is not adequate to the biblical meaning. I recall from my Garrett days how often the Old Testament professor, Charles Kraft, would say that the Old Testament prophets were not "foretellers" but "forthtellers." That is, the prophets spoke about God's will. When the prophets did predict the future it was on the basis of saying that the behavior of the people would have certain consequences in God's world or that God had willed certain things for the people. And when they did predict the future, it always involved the "if." That is, as is clear in the book of Jonah, these things will come to pass *if* you do not change your ways.

In 1 Corinthians, where Paul puts prophecy next to love, it is clear that he is not speaking of some spectacular ability to foretell the future. Prophecy, he tells us, upbuilds people, encourages them, and consoles them (1 Cor. 14:3). In short, prophecy means the proclamation of God's will, the spreading of the gospel. When unbelievers hear prophecy, they may be converted (1 Cor. 14:24). Prophecy includes preaching as we know it in the church, but it is not confined to the pulpit. Wherever any Christian explains the gospel to another person, that is prophecy.

Given this meaning of prophecy, it is significant that

Paul says that it is a gift given only to some Christians (1 Cor. 12:10). A great many faithful Christians find that they are quite incapable of trying to proclaim the gospel to unbelievers. They are usually made to feel inferior and guilty because of this by triumphalists who boast of how they are always proclaiming the gospel to everyone they meet. In fact, in the church today we often identify "witnessing to the faith" with verbally telling people about the faith. But Paul reminds us that not all have received the gift of prophecy that enables them to tell the good news. But it does not follow that those without the gift of prophecy are unable to witness to the faith. Their lives and actions may speak more loudly and be used by God as much or more than the wordiness of those who boast of their ability to tell others.

It is not only to the Corinthians that Paul speaks of the diversity of the gifts. He speaks in a very similar way to the Romans in Chapter 12. Again he affirms the variety of the gifts and again he calls upon his readers not to boast because of their gifts. In doing so, he again uses the analogy of the body with its different members. It is interesting, however, to see that he gives an almost totally different list of the gifts of the Spirit here than he does in 1 Corinthians. Here he mentions service, teaching, exhorting, contributing with liberality, giving aid, and doing acts of mercy. The only gift appearing in both lists is prophecy. One immediately notes that the list of gifts here is less spectacular than the list in 1 Corinthians, and this may be because the Roman congregation had received less spectacular forms than the Corinthians.

As we search through the New Testament we find a host of other things mentioned as gifts of the Spirit. It seems fair to say that the Christians saw no limits to the gifts that God bestowed upon those who believe. Paul could see his celibacy and his "thorn in the flesh" as gifts of the Spirit. Ability to stand in the face of adversity and persecution was a gift of the Spirit. The early Christians were continually expecting ever-new gifts of the Spirit to be manifest among them.

The gifts of the Spirit result in a division of labor in the church. Again, this is no reason to see oneself as exalted over others. Thus in 1 Cor. 12:27ff., Paul lists apostles, prophets, teachers, miracle workers, healers, helpers, administrators, and speakers in tongues. In short, a diversity of gifts is necessary to the working of the church. This particular listing speaks a word to a seminary president. Among the gifts of the Holy Spirit is administration. It is common in the church today to take a rather low view of administration. Pastors complain that they want to preach the gospel, counsel the troubled, and teach the faith. But in reality, they have to spend much of their time administering the life of the congregation. It is well, therefore, to be reminded that administration is as much a gift of the Spirit as these other activities deemed more noble. And good administration is as necessary to the church as are the others.

In summary, boasting is precluded for the Christian

because all gifts come by grace alone, and a wide diversity of gifts is given, with no one receiving all of them. Every Christian is a "charismatic" in that she or he has received gifts from the Spirit. Differences in such gifts are not a sign of some kind of superiority in the spiritual life. Some of the gifts are spectacular and out of the ordinary, but most of them seem to be of a much more ordinary nature. In fact, so ordinary are they that it is easy to overlook the fact that they are gifts of the Spirit. This, no doubt, is why one of the gifts listed is "discernment." The gift of discernment is necessary so that we can discern the act of the Spirit where the undiscerning see only another event. This is how we would expect the manifestation of the Holy Spirit in light of the Incarnation. Even as Jesus was seen by some only as a prophet, or worse as a blasphemer and a criminal, so to some observers the gift of the Spirit are but natural talents of the persons involved. As it took a revelation from God to enable Peter to confess, "You are the Christ" (Matt. 16:16), so the gift of discernment is necessary to see the Holy Spirit at work.

A third form of triumphalism involves seeing the Holy Spirit in terms of gifts to individuals. One of the major features of all triumphalist religions is emphasizing the benefits received by the individual believer. If someone asks, "Why should I accept your religion?" the triumphalist answers in terms of the benefits that the questioner will receive upon entering the religion. We live in an individualistic society, and it is therefore not surprising that we hear a great deal about what Christian faith will do for the individual. I once heard a Roman Catholic priest say that the major heresy of American religion is that we tell people that they ought to be Christians because it will be good for them. This is illustrated by an advertisement placed in the New York subways some years ago which read, "Go to church this Sunday, it will make you feel better." Since triumphalism is so centered on the benefits for the individual, it is not surprising that when triumphalism speaks about the Holy Spirit, it concentrates upon the glories for the individual believer that come from receiving the Holy Spirit.

A theology of the cross reminds us that this centrality of the individual is foreign to the New Testament. When we turn to the New Testament we do find that the individual is important in the eyes of God. But what is central is always the community. In the 12th chapter of 1 Corinthians, at which we have been looking, Paul says, "To each is given the manifestation of the Spirit *for the common good*" (1 Cor. 12:7; italics mine). A gift of the Spirit is not something for the individual to treasure as a personal possession; it is to be shared with the community. In Chapter 14 Paul illustrates this by saying, "He who speaks in a tongue edifies himself, but he who prophesies edifies the church" (1 Cor. 14:4). From this Paul concludes that while he does not want to discourage speaking in tongues, he wants to seek to prophesy because "He who prophesies is greater than he who speaks in tongues, unless someone interprets, so that the church may be edified" (1 Cor. 14:5). Paul goes on to admonish the proud Corinthians, ". . . since you are eager for manifestations of the Spirit, strive to excel in building up the church" (1 Cor. 14:12).

Furthermore, this emphasis upon building up the church is far from a community self-centeredness. The church exists to serve the world and to win unbelievers to itself. Paul brings this out a few verses later when he asks what an outsider will think if he comes into a worship service and hears speaking in a tongue that is unintelligible (1 Cor. 14:16-25). Such a person will obviously not be edified or drawn into the community of the church. But if the unbelieving outsider hears understandable words of prophesy, there is real hope the words will move the outsider to worship God and declare that "God is really among you" (1 Cor. 14:25). The concern for the world is also shown in Paul's listing among the gifts of the Spirit those gifts of service, teaching, contributing with liberality, giving aid, and doing acts of mercy.

The concept that God's gifts are given for the sake of the wider world is a basic biblical theme from beginning to end. In the older covenant, Abraham's descendants are chosen, not simply for their own sakes but so that "all the families of the earth" might be blessed (Gen. 12:3). The Old Testament is always clear that God chose the Jews, not so that they might be exalted, but so that all the nations of the earth might come to worship the God of Abraham, Isaac, and Jacob.

When the Hebraic people became triumphalist in their thinking and expected that being chosen meant that God would play favorites with them, their prophets rebuked them. Amos, for example, speaking for God, says, "You only have I known of all the families of the earth; therefore . . ." and here the triumphalist expects to hear something like, "I will reward you, I will protect you from your enemies, etc." But Amos ends the sentence, "Therefore I will punish you for all your iniquities" (Amos 3:2). Jesus summed up the theme of the Bible when he said, "Everyone to whom much is given, of him will much be required" (Luke 12:48).

A theology of the cross, therefore, will insist that the gifts of the Holy Spirit are given primarily so that the recipient may be of greater service to the church and the world. The triumphalist wants to hear that the Spirit will give him or her rich benefits. Instead, there comes the promise that the Holy Spirit will make us more fruitful for the church and the world.

One of the major works of the Holy Spirit is to bring unity to the church itself. Jude can go so far as to say that those who cause divisions in the church are "devoid of the Spirit" (Jude 19). Perhaps we should not put too much emphasis upon a single verse in an obscure book of the New Testament, but there is much in the New Testament to justify this judgment. Paul's chiding the Corinthians about their boasting of their spiritual gifts was obviously in large part based upon the fact that such boasting was destroying the unity

100

of the church in Corinth. Paul's list of the works of the flesh, at which we have looked, includes enmity, strife, jealousy, and party spirit (Gal. 5:20). Inasmuch as Paul was here contrasting the works of the flesh with the works of the Spirit, it appears that those creating divisions were being branded as devoid of the Spirit, even as Jude says.

The New Testament is much concerned with unity and prizes highly the *koinonia,* that close relationship of love and affection that bound the Christians together. This was seen as the work of the Holy Spirit. Immediately after receiving the Holy Spirit at Pentecost, the church began to own all things in common (Acts 2:44). And so when Paul found that the Corinthians were breaking apart this *koinonia,* he wrote, "For while there is jealousy and strife among you, are you not of the flesh, and behaving like ordinary men?" (1 Cor. 3:3). The sense of loving unity among the people of the church is, therefore, a mark of the Holy Spirit's activity.

Our look at the New Testament emphasis on the Holy Spirit's gifts as being for the sake of the community and the world leads us to agree wholeheartedly with John Koenig. He summed up his study of this theme by saying:

> The New Testament writers propose to measure growth in faith not so much by taking the spiritual pulses of individuals — this is our peculiar Western bias — as by examining what happens in a community and the world immediately surrounding that community. Biblically speaking,

one gauges the number, quality and effectiveness of the spiritual gifts *per congregation*.[2]

Where the concern is first for the building up of the congregation and service to the world, people will be much less likely to be tempted to boast about their particular gifts from the Spirit.

The final form of triumphalism which I am going to treat is that which claims that the Holy Spirit has brought to its recipient a life blissfully free from troubles and a faith so strong that it is always happy and certain. Testimonials of this nature are heard continuously on television, religious shows, and in personal contacts. One result is that many ordinary Christians are filled with a sense of guilt and even despair because they find that their faith is often beset with doubts and their lives are anything but trouble-free. Somehow, they feel, they must be lacking in faith or effort, or they too would share the triumphant faith and life that they hear being reported.

A theology of the cross certainly does not picture the Christian life as being continuously miserable and beset with doubts, but neither does it find any biblical basis for expecting all sunshine and certainty. Consider, for example, Mark's account of Jesus' baptism. First the heavens opened and the Spirit descended upon him (1:10), but two verses later we read "The Spirit immediately drove him out into the wilderness. And he was in the wilderness forty days, tempted by Satan" (1:12-13). This account of Jesus illustrates the profound truth that, with the coming of the Spirit, temptation becomes greater, not less. This is a reality that is witnessed to by the saints down through the ages. Luther, for example, found a never-ceasing battle with temptation as he was continually haunted with the doubt that God could really be gracious to such a miserable sinner as he was.

If we look to the life of Paul, it is obvious that, after his receiving of the Spirit, life was anything but undiluted happiness and good fortune. On several occasions Paul recited to his readers the many adversities that he had faced. They included imprisonments, beatings, stonings, shipwrecks, hunger, and thirst (e.g., 2 Cor. 11:23-29). Furthermore, Paul suffered from a "thorn in the flesh." Scholars have long debated what the problem was. Regardless of what it was, it was a pain that Paul prayed to have removed. But it was not removed, and Paul affirmed that God said to him, "My grace is sufficient for you, for my power is made perfect in weakness" (2 Cor. 12:9). This is a far cry from those triumphalist forms of Christianity which find the Spirit's power only in triumphs and strength. Paul concludes his discussion of his unremoved thorn in the flesh with the paradoxical statement "for when I am weak, then I am strong" (2 Cor. 12:10).

This paradox of Paul runs through the whole New Testament. It was manifest in the incarnation, where God came in the baby in the manger and the man upon a cross. Jesus expressed it when he said, "For whoever would save his life will lose it; and whoever loses his life for my sake and the gospel's will save it" (Mark

8:35). Paul reminded the Christians that not many wise, mighty, or noble persons are to be found in the church because "God chose what is weak in the world to shame the strong" (1 Cor. 1:26-29).

Again and again throughout the New Testament we are told that the Spirit brings joy and peace (e.g., Gal. 5:22), but we do not understand these passages unless we see them in light of this paradox. We read in Phil. 4:7 that the peace of the Christians is one that "passes all understanding." It passes understanding because it does not look like peace to the outsider; it is not the kind of peace the world is seeking. Paul's life, with its imprisonments, beatings, etc., looks anything but peaceful to the world. "If this be peace," says the world, "deliver me from it." And yet the New Testament attests to the paradox that a strange peace is found in the life in the Spirit, not because all troubles have vanished, but because God's presence as the Spirit is known in the midst of all that seems to deny peace.

The joy of which the New Testament speaks is also a joy that passes understanding. Thus Paul could describe life in the Spirit as being "sorrowful, yet always rejoicing" (2 Cor. 6:10). The problem is that we tend to identify joy with what the world calls happiness. Happiness, in the mind of the world, requires a life of pleasure, freed from all troubles. How can we be sorrowful and happy at the same time? But the joy to which the New Testament witnesses is not dependent upon a life free from trouble. In fact, it may be most manifest in times of pain and tragedy. Parish pastors have all had the experience of ministering to a terminally ill person who is suffering great pain. And yet, radiating from that person, they have seen joy. It is the joy that comes from knowing that "neither death, nor life . . . will be able to separate us from the love of God in Christ Jesus our Lord" (Rom. 8:38-39). Perhaps the greatest heresy of triumphalism is that it promises a joy and a peace that are fully understandable. In doing so, it distorts the real promise that comes to us in Scripture.

The Jesus who called his followers to take up their crosses does not lead us into a life of continual euphoria. Harry Emerson Fosdick told about a man who came to him and said that he had become an atheist. "You won't understand this," said the man, "but since becoming an atheist I have been far more happy than when I was a Christian." Fosdick commented that, in fact, he understood this very well. When the Holy Spirit takes hold of us, we feel the burden of all the world's sufferings and ills. We are filled with the ever-frustrating desire to overcome injustice, suffering, and hunger. A world such as ours, with so much injustice and suffering, will always be a pain to the person who has been captured by the spirit of Christ. As Fosdick saw, it could well be a source of happiness for a person to give up Jesus and hence no longer be so moved by the ills about us. Again we are forced back to an understanding of the paradoxical peace and joy that passes all human understanding.

In this paper I have started a process of thinking

about the Holy Spirit in the light of a theology of the cross. In the first place, even as the Word of God became flesh, so the Holy Spirit works in and through this earthly material world in which we live and breathe. In the second place, the Holy Spirit itself and its gifts come to us by grace and hence are no basis for boasting. Thirdly, the Holy Spirit is intimately related to the community. It is to the community that the Holy Spirit comes, and its gifts are meant to build up the community, bringing true unity. And finally, while a theology of the cross does not deny that from the Holy Spirit there come important victories, healings, and successes for which Christians are thankful, there is no guarantee that the Spirit will preserve believers from all ills. On the contrary, often it is in the midst of adversity and tragedy that the enduring presence of the Spirit becomes most real.

As we look back over these insights of a theology of the cross, it becomes apparent to me that a major flaw in all triumphalist views of the Spirit is that all sight is lost of the New Testament affirmation that the Holy Spirit is a pledge and a promise. For example, 2 Cor. 1:22 reads that God "has put his seal upon us and given us his Spirit in our hearts as a guarantee." The New English Bible makes it even clearer by translating the last part "and as a pledge of what is to come has given the Spirit to dwell in our hearts." Eph. 1:14 makes the same point by saying that the Holy Spirit "is the guarantee of our inheritance until we acquire possession of it, to the praise of his glory." In these and many other

New Testament passages, it is clear that the Spirit has been given as God's pledge that the promises of God will be fulfilled. The Spirit and its gifts are the first fruits of what is to come, a foretaste of what God has in store.

The theology of hope quite rightly pointed to the presence throughout the Bible of God's promises. Christian hope looks to a future in which God's promises will be fulfilled. But why should we trust God to keep the promises? One theologian of hope, carried away with the emphasis on looking to the future, went so far as to say that the "present is God-forsaken." If that were the case, what reason would we have for hope in the future? But the New Testament clearly answers this by saying that we may hope for the future because, in the present, the Holy Spirit and its gifts give us a guarantee, a pledge, a foretaste of what is to come.

Triumphalism occurs when people find fulfillment through the Spirit rather than promise of fulfillment. When the Holy Spirit is disassociated from the earthly and physical life in which we live and is identified with a nonmaterial experience, there is an attempt to have heaven, the Kingdom of God, here and now rather than in the future. When the self-acclaimed Spirit-filled person exalts himself or herself over others, there is a sense of having arrived and attained rather than being on the way and moving towards a fulfillment in the future. When the Holy Spirit is individualized and not seen as building up the community, there is the obvious attempt to leave behind the struggling church and find fulfillment for the self. Finally, the idea that the Holy Spirit gives full happiness, success, and triumph in the present is an obvious attempt to have here and now the blessed life that is promised for the future.

The Holy Spirit is God at work in the church and the world today. Without the Holy Spirit the church would be without power and courage to face its trials. The Holy Spirit alone brings people to faith. It is the presence of the Holy Spirit that assures us that God loves us, forgives us, and is with us even when the events of our lives seem to deny all reality of God or of God's love. In the Holy Spirit we do not achieve, here and now, final victory or fulfillment. But because of the Holy Spirit, we have the strength to continue on the way, pressing forward to that which God has promised.

Notes

Chapter 1

1. I must be careful here. We do not need a Spirit-centeredness, but we do need a Spirit-sensitivity. In my zeal to correct unscriptural views of the Spirit, I have sometimes neglected this important New Testament truth.

2. From this point on through Chapter 2 the Bible translations are by the author unless otherwise noted.

3. Dr. Henrietta Mears, the marvelous expositor mentioned just earlier, knew no Greek or Hebrew, but she read her English Bible so voraciously that she penetrated the text as deeply with her spirit as the languages enable one to penetrate it with the mind. If one had to choose between a passionate spirit and a knowledge of the biblical languages, one should, of course, opt for the spirit. But in seminary it is

not necessary to make the invidious choice. Let us seek both.

4. The best Reformation plea for the ministers' knowledge and use of the biblical languages of which I am aware is Luther's impassioned "To the Councilmen of All Cities in Germany that They Establish and Maintain Christian Schools" (1524) in *Luther's Works* (American Edition), 45:357-66. He says, for example, "Although the gospel came and still comes to us through the Holy Spirit alone, we cannot deny that it came through the medium of languages, was spread abroad by that means, and must be preserved by the same means" (pp. 358-359). He also says, "And let us be sure of this: we will not long preserve the gospel without the languages. The languages are the sheath in which this word of the Spirit (Eph. 6:17) is contained; they are the casket in which this jewel is enshrined; they are the vessel in which this wine is held" (p. 360). Especially to the point are the words, "Although faith and the gospel may indeed be proclaimed by simple preachers without a knowledge of languages, such preaching is flat and tame; people finally become weary and bored with it, and it falls to the ground. But where the preacher is versed in the languages, there is a freshness and vigor in his preaching, Scripture is treated in its entirety, and faith finds itself constantly renewed by a continual variety of words and illustrations" (p. 365).

5. The Hebrew word for Spirit in the Old Testament, *ruach,* is in the feminine gender—a "she"; "she" is

preferable to the New Testament's Greek neuter *pneuma*—an "it"—for a variety of reasons.

6. Gerhard Ebeling, *Luther: Einführung in sein Denken* (Tübingen: J.C.B. Mohr [Paul Siebeck], 1964), p. 60.

7. Like the tango, it takes two to preach.

8. The peace and social justice causes, for example, are not extraneous to the cause of the church; they are its lifeblood; they are what the Scriptures so often *say*. Expository preaching—especially of the prophets and the synoptic Gospels—makes churches social. It is the *thematic* preaching of these causes almost exclusively that is so deadening in many liberal-liberationist churches. Churches on the right are too exclusively Pauline (-Johannine); churches on the left are too exclusively prophetic (-synoptic); the people of God need the whole counsel of God to be wholesome and alive. It is a matter, again, of "giving them their *food* [the whole of God's Word] in its *season* [for the whole of God's world]" (Matt. 24:45).

9. Matt. 27:50; Mark 15:37—*exepneusen;* Luke 23:46; John 19:30.

10. E.g., 2 Corinthians 3; Gal. 3:1-5; John 6:63; 15:26-27. Cf. also the whole book of Acts.

Chapter 2

1. Saint Chrysostom, *Homilies on the Gospel of Saint Matthew,* "Nicene and Post-Nicene Fathers," First

Series, ed. Philip Schaff, vol. 10 (Grand Rapids, Mich.: Eerdmans, 1978) 11:7:73.

2. In Matthew, Jesus is also *conceived* by the Spirit (1:18, 20) so that Jesus' baptismal reception of the Spirit (3:16-17) is not his conversion; it is, at one and the same time, his installation into public messianic service—into the office of Christ—and his first specific messianic service to the church: showing it (as Matt. 28:19 also does at the end of the gospel) where the Spirit comes to it, too.

3. Lest the language of baptismal *regeneration* seem too strong, may I refer Reformed Christians especially to authoritative texts in the Reformed tradition (in *The Book of Confessions*) where such language is used or approached: *The Scots Confession* (1560) 21:3.21; *The Second Helvetic Confession* (1566), where we see the words *regeneration* and *regenerated,* 19:5.178-179; 20:5.187; *The Confession of 1967,* 9:51; cf. also the third article of *The Nicene Creed* (381) and questions 69-71 of *The Heidelberg Catechism* (1563).

4. Letter of Donna Holliday (Austin, Texas), March 9, 1982.

Chapter 4

1. See John Koenig, *Charismata: God's Gifts for God's People,* (Philadelphia, The Westminster Press, 1978), p. 54.

2. Ibid., p. 164.